DIVINATION
for Beginners

Quarto.com

© 2023 Quarto Publishing Group USA Inc.
Text © 2018 Liz Dean
Illustrations © 2018 Quarto Publishing Group USA Inc.

First Published in 2023 by New Shoe Press, an imprint of The Quarto Group,
100 Cummings Center, Suite 265-D, Beverly, MA 01915, USA.
T (978) 282-9590 F (978) 283-2742

Essential, In-Demand Topics, Four-Color Design, Affordable Price
New Shoe Press publishes affordable, beautifully designed books covering evergreen, in-demand subjects. With a goal to inform and inspire readers' everyday hobbies, from cooking and gardening to wellness and health to art and crafts, New Shoe titles offer the ultimate library of purposeful, how-to guidance aimed at meeting the unique needs of each reader. Reimagined and redesigned from Quarto's best-selling backlist, New Shoe books provide practical knowledge and opportunities for all DIY enthusiasts to enrich and enjoy their lives.

Visit Quarto.com/New-Shoe-Press for a complete listing of the New Show Press books.

New Shoe Press titles are also available at discount for retail, wholesale, promotional, and bulk purchase. For details, contact the Special Sales Manager by email at specialsales@quarto.com or by mail at The Quarto Group, Attn: Special Sales Manager, 100 Cummings Center, Suite 265-D, Beverly, MA 01915, USA.

ISBN: 978-0-7603-8394-0
eISBN: 978-0-7603-8395-7

The content in this book was previously published in *The Divination Handbook* (Fair Winds Press 2019) and *The Ultimate Guide to Divination* (Fair Winds Press 2018), both by Liz Dean.

Library of Congress Cataloging-in-Publication Data available

Illustration: Mattie Wells

DIVINATION
for Beginners

Simple Techniques for Manifestation and Predicting the Future with Cards, Crystals, and More

LIZ DEAN

NEW SHOE PRESS

"

What you seek is

seeking you.

"

– R U M I

Contents

Introduction 6

1 Divination with Crystals 8

2 Divination with Runes. 28

3 Divination with Tea 48

4 Palmistry 60

5 Divination with Tarot Cards .92

6 Numerology. 124

7 Scrying with a Crystal Ball .136

About the Author 142

Index. 143

A Note about the Future

If you are dipping into divination for the first time, it's important to understand what is meant by future and/or outcome. This is the most likely outcome given present circumstances—which change constantly. A reading suggests the potential future at the time of the reading; the future is not fixed. We have free will, and as we change, so can the future.

Asking Questions for Divination

Before you begin with any divination technique, formulate your question. If the question is right, the answer is more likely to make sense to you. In my work as a tarot teacher and reader, I help people formulate questions that really reflect their situations. The most common request is, "Will he or she come back?" My response is, "Is this really the question?" Most people already know the answer. What they're really seeking is confirmation, and confirmation requires a yes-no response. In divination, it's best to avoid these closed questions. They set a limit on a reading, narrowing it to one answer rather than exploring the myriad possibilities a good reading can offer. Instead, the questioner might ask, "What can make me happy?" or "What do I need to know now?" The answer to their original question will usually arise within the scope of a much broader, more rewarding reading.

Introduction

If you have this book in your hands, you are answering a call to connect with your intuitive wisdom; it's time to explore, find, or reconnect with a divinatory art that resonates with you.

This book presents key tools and techniques for divination: crystal casting and pendulums; runes; tea readings; palmistry; tarot cards; numerology; and crystal ball gazing. These art forms gave our ancestors answers, and they will give you, special insights into the past, present, and future, too.

While it's impossible to cover each one in depth here, I hope that you are inspired to try new practices and gain new insights into those with which you are familiar.

CHAPTER

Divination with Crystals

In a crystal reading, we interpret a group of crystals that fall randomly or are placed in a layout. Interpreting the random fall of crystals is known as stone-casting. You will need a selection of crystals and a reading mat. The crystals listed in this book include many that are commonly used in healing and divination, but this list isn't exclusive; collect crystals that you feel a connection with. Store your crystals wrapped in fabric, such as silk, in a soft bag or purse to protect them.

You can make a mat on which to cast, or gently throw, your crystals by folding a cloth or scarf into a square. Make sure that it is thick enough to protect the crystals when they fall, and release them gently, not too high over the mat, to ensure that any more fragile pieces do not become damaged. The mat is an important part of the reading, because we interpret the positions of the stones on (and off) it, so it is worthwhile to create one that reflects the special ritual of casting stones. For example, you might choose material of a color that helps you feel calm and self-connected, such as blue or purple, rather than a color that shouts for attention.

Crystal Cleansing

Cleansing crystals removes any energies they may have picked up on their journey to you. Use one of the following methods:

- **Water.** Soak your crystals in a bowl of spring water for twenty-four hours for deep cleansing or hold them under a running tap for a few minutes, setting the intention that any negative imprints on them will be washed away. Don't use this method on crystals affected by water, such as selenite, halite, malachite, gypsum, pyrite, optical calcite, or turquoise.

- **Sunlight or moonlight.** Place your crystals outside in sunlight for a few hours, or under moonlight for a few hours or overnight. Don't use sunlight on photosensitive crystals such as amethyst, fluorite, rose quartz, or some calcites. And don't use sunlight for crystal balls, as this is a fire hazard.

- **Incense or smudging.** Waft the smoke from a smudge stick or incense stick over your crystals.

- **Singing bowls or bells.** Place your crystals in a singing bowl and ring the edge with the bowl's mallet to build up the sound, gradually increasing the speed or ring a bell by your crystals; the sound waves will shift any stagnation in them.

- **Breath.** Set your intention for the crystal and gently breathe on its surfaces.

- **White-light visualization.** Visualize the crystal being purified by white light that comes first through you, then into the crystal. See any old, negative energy leave the crystal and disappear.

Attuning to Your Crystals

Hold each crystal in turn. Close your eyes and tune in to its vibration. You will find that you get a warmth and/or tingly feeling as you and your crystal connect. Some people find that their crystal feels freezing cold. If you do not sense a physical change, which indicates a connection with the crystal, or an inner knowing that you are bonding, it's likely that the crystal is not right for you. It may need further cleansing, or to be passed on to someone with whom it connects.

Setting Your Intention

Hold each crystal in turn and say, "I work with this crystal for my highest good and that of others." This intention-setting programs your crystals for the positive work ahead.

Casting the Stones: Techniques

Here's how to cast the stones for a reading:

- Choose a selection of crystals, or if you are reading for another person, ask her to choose the stones from your collection. Place them in the bowl, and tip it onto the mat, as you or she focuses on what you would like to know.

- Rather than use a bowl, shake—or have the querent shake—the crystals with both hands and release them onto the mat, asking a question about or insight into a situation.

- For a past, present, future reading (see page 14), place your crystals in a purse or bag. Put your hand in the bag and, without looking, withdraw three at once, or one at a time.

A Simple Yes-No Reading: Three Crystals

If you have a question that needs a straight answer, choose a black stone, a white stone, and another stone from your collection. Designate the black and white stones as yes and no, or vice versa. The other stone you choose will be the deciding stone—its position in relation to the yes and no stones gives you your answer.

Palm the three stones and then cup both hands together and shake them, thinking of your question.

When you are ready, release the stones onto the mat. Where is the deciding stone? If it is closer to your yes stone, the answer to your question is yes. If it's closer to the no stone, the answer is no. If it is equidistant between yes and no, start again, casting the stones a maximum of three times. If after three tries you cannot obtain an answer, try again another day; the answer is not yet known.

Crystal Insights: Nine or Ten Stones

This reading helps you see the most important issues and decisions around you now. You can use nine or ten stones, or another number that intuitively feels right.

When you are ready, hold your question or inquiry in your mind. You might ask:

- What should I be focusing on now?
- How do I deal with (this) situation?
- What do I need to know?

Place your crystals into a small bowl or shake them in your cupped hands. Release them onto the mat.

- The crystals closest to you, at the front of the mat, show what is at the forefront of your mind; the key issues that need addressing.

- Crystals in the center represent advice from the stones on how to address these concerns.

- Those farthest away from you show what is hidden or distant and may come into play in the future.

- Crystals that land off the mat are disregarded.

- Crystals that are partly on or off the mat are read as events that are coming your way but are not important yet.

Look up the interpretations of each crystal and/or hold each one in turn and see what you pick up intuitively. You might sense a crystal's meaning or its healing potential; you may sense colors or connect with particular memories. Crystals can be conduits to deep insight and/or past-life experiences. Be open to how your crystals communicate with you. Note your impressions.

You will also see that your crystals have formed little groups. Interpret them by what they have in common. For example, moonstone and lapis lazuli traditionally suggest a strong focus on spirituality, intuition, and dreams, so the pair shows the need to be guided by what is otherworldly or subconscious; there might be a message in a dream, or a need to listen carefully to intuitive guidance. As with single stones, you might like to hold groups of crystals and feel if there is a strong, common message or sensation that links them.

Crystal Insights: A Quick Reading

Cast your nine or ten stones onto the mat, but only interpret the three that fall closest to you (take the others off the mat).

Past, Present, Future

This simple reading helps you frame an event in the past, see what is happening in the present, and look at future influences.

Put all your crystals in a bag or purse and draw three, one at a time. Place the first stone on the left, the second stone in the center, and the third stone on the right, in a row:

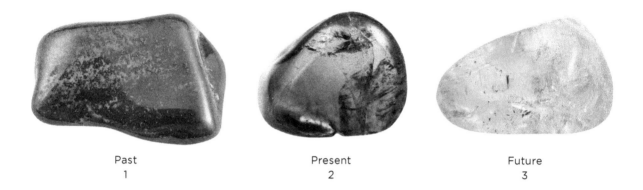

Past
1

Present
2

Future
3

Interpret all three crystals together, but this time, you have the advantage of a timeline. For example, you might have bloodstone, smoky quartz, and citrine (as shown). Bloodstone means resilience, smoky quartz patience and resources, and citrine money and manifesting. In response to the question, "Can my new business idea grow?" one interpretation would be:

"Your business has been hard work (the past); now, you may need to see results, but you need to be patient—you have the resources to hold your position (the present); the successful business you want will come. Keep manifesting this through dedication, and have confidence (future)."

This is based on the traditional meanings of the stones, but you may also use meanings that intuitively arise at the time of your reading. Go with what feels right.

Crystal Meanings in Divination

Here are suggested meanings for crystals used in divination. Over time, you may devise your own personal meanings for your crystal readings.

Agate (various colors)

Divinatory meaning: Success, prosperity

Agate is associated with success and abundance, reaching goals, and being well rewarded. It also shows a connection with the earth and the environment, so it reveals a grounded, can-do attitude. You may find that being in nature helps you replenish and grow emotionally and spiritually.

Agate, blue lace (blue)

Divinatory meaning: News, communication

Communications and news arrive. You may need to express your feelings and ideas sensitively; work out what you need to say to negotiate a delicate situation and avoid misunderstandings. There is support around you.

Agate, fire (red, orange, green, blue)

Divinatory meaning: Secret fears

It is time to express and release buried doubts or fears. Communicating your concerns comes with a risk of rejection, but speaking your truth empowers you. Your words clear away confusion and create an opportunity for future security. Call upon your inner strength to voice your fears.

Agate, moss (green)

Divinatory meaning: Finding treasure

Your treasure may be talents, inner resources, or a desired goal. As this crystal is traditionally known as the gardener's stone, you may find treasure in the earth or discover a relationship with the natural world that inspires your imagination. Trees and rituals that honor the seasons connect you with your Self.

Amazonite (green, blue)

Divinatory meaning: Trust in the universe

Adventures beckon, but worry and anxiety may be blocking your progress. This is unnecessary, as this stone predicts good outcomes in examinations or other tests. Trust yourself. You may be called to divination, clairvoyance, or other creative and compassionate pursuits that rely on clear communication. The work you dream of awaits.

Amber (yellow, orange-yellow)

Divinatory meaning: Protection, potential

Your innate wisdom can say who and what are best for you. You may be considering positive changes to your lifestyle and assessing certain relationships just now; protect yourself from any negativity or friendships that drain you. Amber is also a stone of potential—there's a light within you that is ready to shine.

Amethyst (purple)

Divinatory meaning: Spirituality

Amethyst is a stone of intuition that acknowledges spiritual awareness; you may be involved in compassionate work, such as healing, or be ready to develop your intuitive abilities; a creative project may help you deepen your spiritual connection. The stone can also indicate stress and the need to recharge physically and emotionally.

Aquamarine (blue-green)

Divinatory meaning: Perspective

Take a step back and look again. A situation may not be perfect, but with a new perspective, you may see that it is good enough. In relationships, aquamarine is associated with reconnection, so a love bond is repaired or deepened. The stone also suggests travel and protection on your journey, particularly over water.

Aventurine, green

Divinatory meaning: Luck, success

Aventurine brings wealth, harmony, and an opportunity to take the lead. With new responsibility come calculated risks, but luck will be on your side and you'll enjoy success. The stone can also show a need for healing and rebalancing; know that peaceful times are coming. A stressful situation will soon be over.

Bloodstone (aka heliotrope; green-red)

Divinatory meaning: Resilience

A crystal of courage, consistency, and resilience, bloodstone asks you to keep going. Draw upon your energy and wisdom, be relentless, and you can achieve your purpose. You may need to protect yourself from ill health by conserving your energy or to guard against unfair criticism you give or receive. Better communication is always possible.

Carnelian, orange/red

Divinatory meaning: Risk, self-belief

Take a risk and you will succeed. You intuitively know what to do; just listen to your inner guidance. If you feel stressed and blocked, muster your self-confidence and take that leap of faith. Carnelian's positivity also embraces legal decisions, negotiations, agreements, and any decision that means giving yourself more of what you need to live life in balance.

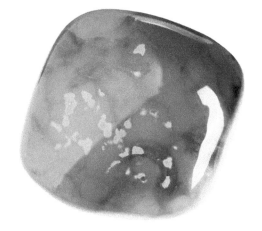

Celestite, blue/white

Divinatory meaning: Angelic messages

Celestite is the stone of heaven, and it can reveal a spiritual connection; you may receive messages from angels and Spirit and feel angels' unconditional love and guidance through synchronicities and unexpected help from those around you. This crystal also suggests imagination, dream recall, and messages through dreams.

Citrine (yellow, yellow-brown)

Divinatory meaning: Manifesting, money

This stone of prosperity and communication gives you a "yes" to any question you might ask in a reading. It also predicts money, sales, and material comforts, which in turn lift your confidence and mood. Citrine also tells you that now is the right time to manifest, with good intentions, whatever you want.

Emerald (green)

Divinatory meaning: Promises

Emerald reveals commitment, so a confidence or promise is kept. In relationships, you speak the truth and honor your own truth. The stone is also linked with finding and retaining information, so you may be researching or studying a subject close to your heart. Additional meanings include success, happiness, and fertility.

Garnet, red

Divinatory meaning: Emotional balance

Love, passion, anger: Powerful emotions abound. You may need to make a personal sacrifice to regain your balance or make peace. Commitment is important to you now. Garnet can also show either a new romance, or in existing partnerships, a temporary separation due to circumstance rather than choice.

Jade, green (aka nephrite, jadeite)

Divinatory meaning: Love

Jade is a stone of love, romance, and compassion. Relationships are central to your life just now, and you take a heart-centered approach beyond personal partnerships, showing kindness to those who do not love themselves enough. Additional meanings include luck and well-being.

Jasper, red

Divinatory meaning: Intensity

You may need to deal with intense emotions such as anger, guilt, or jealousy; these emotions may be yours, or expressed by someone close to you. Step back from the maelstrom and you will see what to do and what not to do. With new insight, a situation or relationship can be restored or rescued.

Jasper, yellow

Divinatory meaning: Blocks

Yellow jasper can reveal blocks to your progress: an energetic block that has a physical impact, such as low energy, low mood, and poor motivation; a creative block, when projects and ideas feel stuck; or feeling, generally, disconnected from spiritual or inner guidance. You may need to release yourself from pressure to perform or to be a certain way to get back in the flow. Yellow jasper can also mean a travel opportunity.

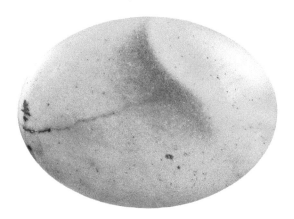

Jet (black)

Divinatory meaning: Endings

Jet says you may be holding on to powerful or negative feelings that need to be released. A situation has ended, and you search for stability during this transition period; this will come as you allow the emotions to arise and, when you are ready, let them go. Jet is also linked with psychic protection and psychic connection.

Labradorite (aka spectrolite; black, blue, yellow iridescent)

Divinatory meaning: Change

Your expectations are shifting. Someone is not as they seem, so be discerning, as what you are told may be exaggerated or false. Protect yourself from other people's negative energies. The stone can also show news and creative skills that bring success. Expect great changes.

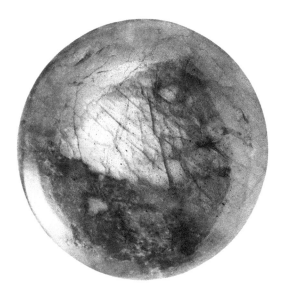

Lapis lazuli (blue, gold)

Divinatory meaning: Insights

Lapis, the heavenly stone, brings insights in dreams and reaffirms your spiritual connection. You may be recalling someone from the past and questioning your relationship with them, seeing this person in a new light; if so, it is time to express your thoughts. A stone of truth, lapis lazuli supports the intellect and guides you to stand up for what you believe in.

Malachite (green)

Divinatory meaning: Challenges, creativity

Trouble is averted; you manage a challenging person or situation and discover not only who your friends are, but your knack for an inventive solution. Partnerships and creative projects thrive, and you may sense a deep, subconscious guidance. Malachite can also mean money.

Moonstone (white, yellow, cream, blue, green)

Divinatory meaning: Harmony, friendship

Moonstone brings harmony, new friends, openness, and flexibility. It is linked with sensitivity, intuition, and dreams, and it can show issues beneath the surface that you are ready to deal with; an old situation may be transformed. A new idea or plan may also be emerging.

Obsidian, Apache tear (black)

Divinatory meaning: Grief

Apache tear denotes dealing with grief, frustration, and fear. You may feel you have little or no control over events and feel vulnerable and highly sensitive. The message, however, is that you are protected and can recover a sense of security. The stone is also associated with psychic protection.

Obsidian, black

Divinatory meaning: Hidden influences, revelations

Obsidian shows you may be acknowledging strong emotions or hidden influences that, if released, can bring positive change. Clearing these past issues may need a slow, gentle approach. Additional meanings include sacred contracts, karmic lessons, cutting attachment ties, and divination.

Onyx (black, gray, blue, white, yellow, brown, red)

Divinatory meaning: Inner wisdom

There may be something you've had to learn or are in the process of learning the hard way, which has brought confusion and even panic. Onyx says you are in a stronger position than you think. Turn inward and connect with your personal power; be self-contained and follow your inner guidance.

Opal, blue

Divinatory meaning: A wish come true

Opal magnifies ideas and increases emotions, ideas, and sensitivity, reassuring you that you can manifest your wishes. You may experience a creative surge and enter a dreamy, imaginative phase that offers new insights. This stone is also connected with clairvoyant ability, and an additional meaning is loyalty.

The following opal colors have these meanings:
Opal, fire: Hopes
Opal, pink: Wish for psychic connection

Peridot, green (aka chrysolite, olivine)

Divinatory meaning: Self-reliance

Disappointment leads to a recognition of your worth. A relationship may not be what you had hoped, but you fortify yourself from within; you may assert your identity and creativity doing work that you love. A particular skill or talent brings you deserved rewards.

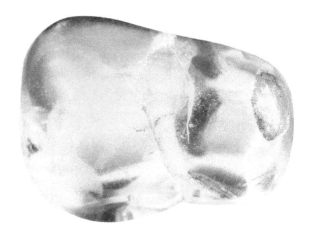

Quartz, clear

Divinatory meaning: Powerful clarity

Clear quartz brings the ability to manifest what you want and build upon what you have, following and knowing your true purpose. A new journey begins, and major changes await. You are protected while you follow your path, and you are blessed with clarity; you will see exactly where you need to go.

Quartz, rose (pink)

Divinatory meaning: Love, reconciliation

The love crystal, rose quartz, brings you a new relationship and an opportunity to heal the old wounds of your heart. Self-love and self-esteem flourish, and you share love unconditionally with others. You receive loving support in your endeavors. An additional meaning is forgiveness.

Quartz, rutilated (aka angel hair; golden/dark strands)

Divinatory meaning: Inspiration

You are inspired to take an idea a step further or leap into a new creative venture. Your insights multiply and you feel connected spiritually, while making new connections with people as your network expands. Rutilated quartz also sees you analyzing a situation from all angles.

Quartz, smoky (yellow, brown)

Divinatory meaning: Patience

Smoky quartz predicts a quiet phase when things move slowly. The changes you want to see will happen, but gradually, when the timing is right. You may feel a need to retreat to conserve your energy, to withdraw so you can recharge. Be patient and all will become clear.

Rhodonite (pink, red)

Divinatory meaning: Sharing

Rhodonite brings the gift of love and sees you finding
your true passion in life. This may be expressed within a
relationship or in acts of service, from showing compassion for
others to teaching or healing. You are now in a position not
only to attract love but to discover your deepest motivations.

Selenite, white

Divinatory meaning: Fixing instability

This stone of spiritual connection says you may have to make
changes to create more security for yourself. This may mean you
see what or who is supportive now and what must stay in the past;
you will gently be able to let go of what you no longer need. New
horizons beckon.

Sodalite (blue)

Divinatory meaning: The right words

Sodalite is a stone of communication, so it is time to express your
ideas. You may need to find a way to translate a concept into plain
language, or in relationships, speak the truth as you see it. The stone
can show problems being solved and a determination to break new
ground.

Sunstone (yellow, orange, brownish)

Divinatory meaning: Being of service

Sunstone shows you are manifesting wealth and abundance; conscious of your worth, you know the contribution you can make. You are warm toward others who need your help, so you may be of service, sharing your wisdom and offering leadership. If you have been through a testing time, sunstone reassures you that all will be well.

Tiger's eye, brown-gold

Divinatory meaning: Evidence

The stone of energy, protection, and confidence, tiger's eye asks you to go beyond appearances to discover the true nature of an issue; look for the evidence beneath the surface glimmer. You call upon your inner strength to see what is hidden and make a decision that protects your interests. Additional meanings include prosperity and happiness.

The following varieties of tiger's eye have these meanings:
Tiger's eye, blue: Relief from anxiety
Tiger's eye, red: Motivation; feeling overwhelmed; need for balance

Tourmaline, black

Divinatory meaning: Focus, protection

Protect yourself from negativity and be aware of any negative thought patterns. Attend to what is important to you. Be resilient and stay grounded and in the present. You don't need to close down to protect yourself, however; you can stay open to the good things in life within safe boundaries. It could also mean a situation coming to an end.

Other varieties of tourmaline have these meanings:
Tourmaline, green: Growth, results
Tourmaline, pink: Compassion, love, beginnings

Turquoise

Divinatory meaning: Prosperity, protection

Turquoise is traditionally a stone of prosperity and protection. In divination, it asks you to guard your possessions and deflect negativity. You may need to tackle tasks you have been avoiding to clear the way for the success that awaits you. Turquoise can also show productivity and creative skill, and it predicts journeys.

CHAPTER

2

Divination with Runes

The runes, a sequence of literal and symbolic letters, are the ancient sacred alphabet of the Germanic peoples of northern Europe. As Germanic languages developed, so did the runes; thus, we have variations in letter formation and the number of runes in a set, or Futhark. Futhark is an acronym after the first six letters of the runic alphabet: Fehu, Uruz, Thurisaz, Ansuz, Raido, and Kaunaz.

Types of Rune to Buy or Make

Futharks are commonly available in natural stone, lightweight fiberglass, wood, ceramic, and crystal; some diviners use cards with runic inscriptions, but many prefer the feel of natural materials and purchase them from independent craftspeople. Traditionally, the runic letters are painted red.

You can make your own runes by painting or wood-burning the letters on pebbles or on pieces of found wood from a fruit-bearing tree. The pieces don't have to be uniform or cut to a regular size, but they will need to be smaller than your palm for easy handling and laying out. Using a knife, carefully pare away some of the bark so you have a surface for your inscription.

What of the blank rune, Wyrd? Although there is no historical evidence for the existence of a blank rune, and its meaning is covered by Pertho (see page 38), some rune sets include it to represent the unknown, or "wyrd." If you have a blank rune in your set, you can use it or ignore it. If you choose to use it, give some thought to how you might interpret it, given the overlap with Pertho. One approach is to assign it as "the answer to [my] question is unknown at this time," or simply as "silence," perhaps advice from the runes to stay silent on the matter in question.

The Elder Futhark

The Elder Futhark of twenty-four runes is arranged in three sets of eight, or aetts. They are named Frey, Hagalaz, and Tyr.

Frey's Aett: Creation and productivity
- Frey's eight deals with fertility and the world's creation.
- Fehu, Uruz, Thurisaz, Ansuz, Raido, Kaunaz, Gebo, Wunjo

Hagalaz's Aett: Disruption and fate
- Hagalaz's eight denotes disruption and the workings of destiny.
- Hagalaz, Nauthiz, Isa, Jera, Eihwaz, Pertho, Algiz, Sowelo

Tyr's Aett: Values and relationships
- Tyr's aett deals with the material world, social values, and relationships.
- Tiwaz, Berkana, Ehwaz, Mannaz, Laguz, Inguz, Othila, Dagaz

RUNE	LETTER	MEANING	INTERPRETATION

Frey's Aett

RUNE	LETTER	MEANING	INTERPRETATION
Fehu	F	Cattle	Prosperity, value, status
Uruz	U	Aurochs	Strength, courage, resilience
Thurisaz	Th	Giant	Defense, attack
Ansuz	A	God	Inspiration, communication
Raido	R	Ride	Journeys, travel, progress
Kaunaz	K	Torch	Inner wisdom, guidance, knowledge
Gebo	G	Gift	Gifts and generosity
Wunjo	W	Joy	Fulfillment of wishes, blessings

Hagalaz's Aett

RUNE	LETTER	MEANING	INTERPRETATION
Hagalaz	H	Hail	Loss or hardship before gain
Nauthiz	N	Need	Restriction and desire
Isa	I	Ice	Blocks, delay, self-preservation
Jera	J/Y	Year, harvest	Time, karma, growth, profit
Eihwaz	Ei	Yew	Life cycles, endings, defense
Pertho	P	Dice cup	Mysteries, the unknown
Algiz	Z	Elk, elk sedge	Growth, protection, higher self
Sowelo	S	Sun	Success, expansion, power

Tyr's Aett

RUNE	LETTER	MEANING	INTERPRETATION
Tiwaz	T	Star, the god Tyr	Bravery, tests, justice, victory, guidance
Berkana	B	Birch	Beginnings, fertility, growth, creativity, outcomes
Ehwaz	E	Horse	Travel, cooperation, trust
Mannaz	M	Mankind	Assessment, decisions, community
Laguz	L	Water	Intuition, clairvoyance, emotions
Inguz	Ng	The god Ing	Protection, fertility, development
Othila	O	Homestead, land	Home and family, comfort, stability
Dagaz	D	Day	New start, optimism, realizations

Frey's Aett

FEHU

MEANING: Cattle, wealth
INTERPRETATION: Prosperity, value, status, power, creative force
LETTER SOUND: F

URUZ

MEANING: Aurochs
INTERPRETATION: Strength, courage, resilience, challenges, health, healing
LETTER SOUND: U

Fehu is the rune of material wealth, and it signifies money flowing through trade: negotiation, contracts, and social transactions that bring profit. As wealth accrued often leads to respect and reputation, your professional and personal networks expand and the results you achieve bring positive attention. At home, you may be focused on practical matters: driving a business forward or forging ahead with creative or personal projects.

There is also a sense of accountability with Fehu, as prosperity can mean sacrifices: Is the price you pay for success justified? While you are working hard toward a goal, be sure your investment of time brings you the personal empowerment you desire and that the value of your work aligns with who you are.

Overall, Fehu brings an opportunity to review and appreciate your achievements. You may share your good fortune with others in the spirit of generous support.

INVERTED MEANING: Financial worries; losing value.

Uruz is the rune of strength and resilience. It represents our primal ability to survive and thrive. Uruz asks you to live fearlessly, to realize your power to create change, and to react to challenges or opposition with courage and self-belief. This rune can also be reassurance that you will overcome obstacles with patience and standing your ground, and by paying close attention to your reactions to conflict. It may mean confronting your fear of failure or of success or overcoming irritation and anger; the battle may be within you. With determination and willpower, you succeed.

Uruz offers the physical strength of the auroch, so it can reveal a recovery from illness or stress and, overall, vital health and well-being.

INVERTED MEANING: Being too domineering; abuse of power.

THURISAZ

MEANING: Giant

INTERPRETATION: Defense, attack, chaos, protection, resistance

LETTER SOUND: Th

ANSUZ

MEANING: Ancestor/god

INTERPRETATION: Inspiration, communication, divine intelligence

LETTER SOUND: A

Thurisaz signifies life's disruption. Yet this rune also invites us to confront this turbulence with courage. It is possible to limit the damage, to guard ourselves from further danger, to protect others in our care, and to fight if necessary. You may experience Thurisaz as an attack on your beliefs or a threat to your position or security. As the rune is also associated with the thorn tree, it affords you protection.

Thurisaz can also represent the darker, shadow side of human nature that we suppress and keep out of conscious sight. A secret may come to light.

INVERTED MEANING: Irritation rather than upheaval.

Ansuz suggests that knowledge is not solely about our personal advancement. Words and knowledge are power, and they create conditions for change; the way we communicate can powerfully affect others and ourselves. In this sense, Ansuz may be using us to express ourselves mindfully. In personal projects, you may be inspired to talk, write, draw, craft, compose, or otherwise manifest ideas. Spiritually, the rune shows you connecting with divine intelligence.

Ansuz represents order and resourcefulness. This rune's meaning of "ancestor" also suggests family connections, ancestral patterns, and past lives. Fehu, the rune of wealth and growth, has two upward strokes, whereas the rune of Ansuz has two downward strokes, suggestive of the past.

INVERTED MEANING: Miscommunication.

RAIDO

MEANING: Ride

INTERPRETATION: Journeys, travel, progress, spiritual path

LETTER SOUND: R

KAUNAZ (KANO)

MEANING: Torch

INTERPRETATION: Inner wisdom, guidance, knowledge, light

LETTER SOUND: K or hard C

ELEMENT: Fire

Raido is the rune of travel. Raido sees you traveling physically or taking an inner journey, perhaps through spiritual development or through education, discovering new territory and gaining fresh insights through new experiences. You make progress by taking charge of your journey and moving in the right direction at a pace that is right for you, rather than being led by others' motivations or ego. Equally, you may need self-discipline and willpower to stay focused. Overall, this travel rune shows making decisions and taking action toward an important goal.

INVERTED MEANING: Procrastination; panic.

Kaunaz is the rune of guidance and inner light. It brings intuition, wisdom, and the passing on of knowledge. It reveals a personal journey to wisdom through learning and, spiritually, the quest for enlightenment. You may be drawn to teaching, training, or mentoring, or you may otherwise find yourself in a position to give advice or relate history through stories.

Kaunaz can also reveal latent talents and abilities and help you make connections; you may see hidden opportunities or inventive ways to solve a problem. You call upon your intuition and your intellect to find what you are looking for.

INVERTED MEANING: Disinterest; ignorance.

GEBO

MEANING: Gift

INTERPRETATION: Gifts, generosity, balance, reciprocity

LETTER SOUND: G

WUNJO

MEANING: Joy

INTERPRETATION: Fulfillment of wishes, blessings, security

LETTER SOUND: W

Gebo is the rune of balance and fairness, of giving and receiving in equal measure. It can predict a gift coming to you or show you being generous to others. This may be the giving of time, giving love to a partner or children, or dedicating oneself to a cause. Gebo also asks you to consider the value of balance and equality and to be able not only to give but to receive gifts with grace, no matter how small. Receiving requires an attitude of surrender, to be comfortable being a passive recipient rather than the active giver.

There is also an aspect of justice in Gebo, in that it speaks of honoring obligations and agreements and committing to what you can reasonably deliver. In this way, the rune supports your need to manage your time, energy, and finances, keeping life in balance. Spiritually, Gebo suggests sacred contracts and karma.

Gebo has no inverted meaning.

Wunjo, the rune of joy and bliss, brings completion and fulfillment. This bliss is the appreciation of material and emotional security, rather than the bliss we often associate with spiritual nonattachment. Your hopes and wishes are granted, and your efforts rewarded.

To get to this place of serenity, you may have to overcome great obstacles or endure pressure and frustration. Battles are done, and it is now time to enjoy your successes and share them with others. Wunjo also has the connotation of unity, showing closeness and cooperation in families, friendship groups, and your wider social circles.

INVERTED MEANING: Feeling disconnected.

Hagalaz's Aett

HAGALAZ

MEANING: Hail

INTERPRETATION: Loss or hardship before gain; transformation

LETTER SOUND: H

ELEMENT: Ice

NAUTHIZ

MEANING: Need

INTERPRETATION: Restriction and desire

LETTER SOUND: N

ELEMENT: Fire

Hagalaz is the rune of transformation. This is fate, or destiny—the Norse wyrd at work. However, the rune asks you to endure hardship because it will lead to positive change. Hagalaz advises you to accept the cycles of bad and good fortune, let go of blame, and see the bigger picture beyond day-to-day difficulties. You may also call upon your past experience to help you endure current challenges; you look to your personal history for answers, or to past incarnations.

This rune is associated with channeling and the underworld realm of the goddess Hel; Hagalaz is also the rune of the mother, so the rune may symbolize the unconscious realm where the dark goddess within us lives. Shadow work or spirit communication may be calling you now. This rune's shape, two parallel lines joined by two strokes, suggests this world and the otherworld, or the conscious and unconscious selves.

Hagalaz has no inverted meaning.

Nauthiz's meaning of "need" suggests "want": When this rune appears in a reading, we may want what we cannot have. We may feel frustrated and restricted. To make a difficult situation bearable, Nauthiz asks that we live in the present moment and attend to practicalities, an idea expressed in the rune's element of fire.

An additional meaning of this rune is desire and passion, and the need for sex and intimacy.

Nauthiz has no inverted meaning.

ISA

MEANING: Ice

INTERPRETATION: Blocks, delay, self-preservation

LETTER SOUND: I (pronounced ee, as in *even*)

ELEMENT: Ice

JERA

MEANING: Year, harvest

INTERPRETATION: Time, karma, growth, profit

LETTER SOUND: J or Y

Isa, the ice rune, represents a blocked or static situation. You may be in control of these conditions, so the rune asks you if you are willing to, for example, look for other routes to your goal. You may need to revise your expectations regarding the timescale of a project or find a way to improve communication in your personal and professional dealings. If this situation is not of your making, use this waiting time as an opportunity for reflection until the blocks dissolve. And there can be value in forced delay; there just might be a gem of an opportunity here that you would otherwise have missed.

Isa also signifies tradition and established values. Ice preserves, and symbolically it preserves the status quo. If you are trying to break new ground, you may find others resist your desire for change.

Isa has no inverted meaning.

Jera is the rune of time. It speaks of right timing—waiting for the right time to push forward and the right time to hold back and rest. This takes experience, patience, and trusting your intuition; to say yes when it feels right to do so, taking on new projects or embarking on new relationships when you sense a positive energetic flow, rather than assenting to offers because they make logical sense. Everything has its own rhythm, so it is now time to attune to your internal energy so work, love, projects, and finances flow.

This rune is also associated with summer and harvest, when the earth provides for all. This also evokes the concept of karma: reaping what you sow. What you have faithfully invested in will bear fruit in good times.

Jera has no inverted meaning.

EIHWAZ
(EIWAZ, EITHWAZ)

MEANING: Yew tree

INTERPRETATION: Life cycles, endings, necessary defense

LETTER SOUND: Ei (*ay* sound)

PERTHO
(PERTHRO, PERTH)

MEANING: Dice cup

INTERPRETATION: Mysteries, the unknown

LETTER SOUND: P

Eihwaz, or yew, stands for the ancient, sacred tree that signifies life, death, and rebirth. In a reading, this rune can reveal endings and losses that are unavoidable, but we must try to accept them so that new life, or possibilities, can awaken.

Eihwaz is also associated with protection and famed for its hardiness and iron-like wood. It asks you to be mindful of your boundaries and defend yourself physically and spiritually when necessary.

Eihwaz has no inverted meaning.

Pertho is the rune of mystery. It reminds us that outcomes are not fixed. You can change your perceived destiny and see the process of divination as a way to empower yourself with choice. It symbolizes the birth of possibilities and traditionally can also indicate the birth of a child.

Overall, Pertho speaks of the inner self and intuition, the parts of us that become activated by the process of divination. An additional meaning is secrets and the need for discretion, to keep your own counsel and listen to that inner voice.

INVERTED MEANING: Feeling disempowered or needlessly anxious.

ALGIZ

MEANING: Elk, elk sedge

INTERPRETATION: Growth, protection, spiritual connection, higher self

LETTER SOUND: Z

SOWELO (SOWELA, SOWILO)

MEANING: Sun

INTERPRETATION: Success, expansion, power

LETTER SOUND: S

ELEMENT: Fire

Algiz takes us into higher realms and the higher self. In a rune reading, it can suggest spiritual development, growth, and protection. It also suggests surrendering to the forces of nature, staying open to possibilities, and accepting that challenges are a necessary part of our learning.

INVERTED MEANING: Extreme defensiveness; being too quick to judge or react.

Sowelo is a rune of optimism and success, bringing the healing and energizing powers of the sun. The form of Sowelo is a lightning bolt, which connects the sky and the earth. This blast of cosmic power awakens us to our purpose and revitalizes but can also destroy whatever is untrue or outdated. In a rune-cast, Sowelo says that you will see results.

Spiritually, this rune represents oneness, a feeling of connection with the earth, and being part of a greater whole. Combine the meaning of Sowelo with Raido, ride (see page 34), and we have Raido's willpower aligned with the higher forces and higher self, suggesting powerful personal growth.

Sowelo has no inverted meaning.

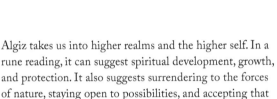

Tyr's Aett

TIWAZ (TEIWAZ)

MEANING: Star; the god Tyr

INTERPRETATION: Bravery, tests, justice, victory, guidance

LETTER SOUND: T

BERKANA

MEANING: Birch

INTERPRETATION: Beginnings, birth, fertility, growth, creativity, outcomes

LETTER SOUND: B

The arrow form of Tiwaz suggests a weapon. In a reading, this rune foretells a battle and asks us to look at the process of success: how we get there, rather than winning at any cost. Tiwaz also means guidance. In the Anglo-Saxon rune poem, this rune is described as "a guiding star," a rune that "is ever on its course over the mists of night and never fails." This tells us to always have hope and self-belief, to keep the faith even when we cannot see the outcome or lose sight of our purpose in the mists of doubt. Support is there.

INVERTED MEANING: Giving up too soon.

Berkana is the rune of creativity and fertility: giving birth to and nurturing children or creative projects. As the birch is also one of the first trees to come into leaf, it represents all spring has to offer: new life, vitality, and possibility. This rune also means protection. When Berkana arrives in a rune-cast, relationships thrive and your projects beautifully unfold.

INVERTED MEANING: Stuckness, lack of growth, creative blocks.

EHWAZ

MEANING: Horse

INTERPRETATION: Travel, flexibility, cooperation, trust, friendship

LETTER SOUND: E (short e as in *get*)

MANNAZ

MEANING: Mankind

INTERPRETATION: Assessment, decisions, community

LETTER SOUND: M

Ehwaz encompasses all journeys and shows you may take a physical trip. There is a strong spiritual dimension to this rune, as it also indicates shamanic journeying or astral travel.

When Ehwaz arrives in a reading, expressing your basic, instinctual needs may be particularly important. It indicates strong, rewarding relationships with others close to you and within the broader community and is a signifier of harmony in your interactions with others.

INVERTED MEANING: Misplaced trust.

Mannaz is the rune of discernment, choices, and humankind. It brings perspective and helps us see ourselves and our communities as part of a greater scheme. Humanity also implies a balanced, humane attitude; we may need to forgive or at least be aware of our faults and have compassion for others' shortcomings in the spirit of friendship and support.

This rune's form, which is Wunjo and its mirror image, can signify Wunjo's meaning of "gift" twice: giving and receiving, or the give-and-take upon which good relationships depend. It advises taking a reasoned rather than intuitive approach to a situation. If you have a key decision to make, take a close look at the facts before making a commitment.

INVERTED MEANING: Narrow-mindedness; hastiness.

LAGUZ

MEANING: Water

INTERPRETATION: Intuition, higher realms, clairvoyance, emotions, collective unconscious

LETTER SOUND: L

ELEMENT: Water

INGUZ (INGWAZ)

MEANING: The god Ing (Yngvi)

INTERPRETATION: Protection, fertility, development

LETTER SOUND: Ng (as in *sing*)

Laguz is associated with emotions, love, and the flow of life. This rune is a symbol of initiation. In a rune-cast, Laguz can reveal you are about to experience a new lease of life and perhaps to be initiated into something new.

Overall, Laguz advises you not to stagnate or hesitate. Immerse yourself in the present, connect with that undercurrent of intuition, and follow it freely.

INVERTED MEANING: Procrastination; self-doubt.

In a rune-cast, the god Ing brings the seeding of ideas, virility, and growth in relationships. This rune's symmetrical shape indicates completeness and fulfillment; the central diamond suggests containment and protection. Ing's form is the double of Gebo, the rune of gifts—gifts of the earth (sustenance) and the gift of new life (fertility).

Ing also reveals spiritual guidance and balance. The two open triangles at the top and bottom of the rune suggest the same internal space as the inner diamond, showing that the external world of matter is given the same consideration as the inner realm; the conscious and unconscious selves are given equal attention.

Inguz has no inverted meaning.

OTHILA (OTHALA)

MEANING: Homestead, land

INTERPRETATION: Generations, ancestors, home and family, comfort, stability

LETTER SOUND: O

DAGAZ

MEANING: Day

INTERPRETATION: A new start, optimism, realizations

LETTER SOUND: D

ELEMENT: Fire

Othila is the rune of family and inheritance. This may be what we inherit physically or materially from family, skills or character traits our parents passed on to us, or knowledge we have accrued from the wisdom traditions we follow. When Othila appears in a rune-cast, you may be focusing on home and relationships, feeling a deeper connection with your family and a sense of belonging right where you are. Othila also stands for material wealth.

Othila suggests strong foundations and the protection that material wealth and strong bonds between people bring. In terms of creative projects, this rune shows an idea that is well conceived; in relationships, Othila shows stability and togetherness.

INVERTED MEANING: Being stuck in the past; insecurity.

Dagaz represents new beginnings and cycles. Spiritually, it can show awareness of other realities, a cosmic consciousness. Dagaz also brings hope and improvement, reminding us that "tomorrow is another day"; we can start over with renewed optimism. As the Anglo-Saxon rune poem says, Day is "beloved of men, a source of hope and happiness to rich and poor, and of service to all."

Dagaz has no inverted meaning.

Reading the Runes

Before you begin a rune reading, find a clean surface, a white cloth (a symbol of pure intention), and a quiet moment. Prepare yourself as you would for any divination ritual: Take a few deep breaths and try to empty your mind of any distractions. Set the intention that your reading will be for the highest good, and when you are ready, allow your question to form. Then you have two options:

- **Place the runes in a set layout.** Choose the runes from the bag as you ponder your question and place them in a layout, all faceup. If any are upside down, you can read the inverted and upright meanings.

- **Cast them onto the cloth.** Choose the runes from the bag as you ponder your question, then cast them, letting them gently fall. You interpret the meanings from their positions on the cloth—whether they are in the center or outside, for example. Facedown runes indicate the future.

Upright and Inverted Meanings

Some runes have an inverted meaning along with an upright meaning. Noninvertible runes are those that have symmetrical forms, so they look the same upright and inverted. You can read the inverted meaning if the rune falls inverted. However, I advise that you read both the upright and inverted meanings and intuit your own "shadow" meaning, as the inverted meanings alone can be rather direct.

The Three Norns

The Norns were the Norse goddesses of Fate who decided the fates of gods and men. The three runes represent Urd (Wyrd), goddess of the past, Verdandi, goddess of the present, and Skuld, goddess of the future. Traditionally, these three runes are read from right to left, beginning with the future and working backward, but you can intuitively choose to read the runes your own way.

Choose three runes from your bag and place them as shown:

1	**2**	**3**
Urd: The past.	Verdandi: The present.	Skuld: The future.

The Decision Reading: Five Runes

This layout uses a cross formation and is helpful for decision making, as it examines the issue in detail and offers a rune that represents the lesson that your situation offers.

Choose five runes from your bag and place them as shown below:

3

What
supports you.

2   **5**   **4**

Potential challenges.   The final outcome and   The immediate outcome.
                         the lesson learned.

1

The influence of the past.

The Nine-Rune Cast

This is a free-form reading, in which you choose nine runes randomly from the bag and gently drop them onto a white cloth or surface. If any fall facedown, leave them until the end of the reading, as these represent the future.

First, look at the runes in the center of the cloth. These represent priorities—the issues or situations that are important to you now—and can reveal hidden influences that may be affecting you.

Secondly, look at any runes that have fallen near the edges of the cloth. These represent how other people may be influencing you or your situation. Ignore any runes that lie outside the area of your cloth.

Finally, look at the facedown runes, turning them faceup but keeping them in the same position on the cloth. These represent the future.

Now look at how the runes in your reading form small groups. Interpret these groups together. It's also helpful to look up the elements associated with some runes on page 31. For example, if a fire rune and an ice rune were close to one another, this suggests tension, given that ice and fire are elemental opposites.

The Grid of Destiny

This reading is a development of the past, present, future method of the Three Norns (see page 44), showing you the influence of friends and family, and it includes a rune that reveals the spiritual perspective on your situation.

If you are reading for another person, he or she chooses eight runes from the bag, and you, as the reader, choose the ninth.

7

Spiritual matters.

8

Friends.

9

Outcome. Chosen by the rune master or mistress.

4

The past.

5

Family.

6

What helps or hinders you.

1

The Significator. Represents you or the querent.

2

Inner self.

3

Goals.

CHAPTER

3

Divination with Tea

Tea leaf reading as a divinatory art has been handed down from mother to daughter, an unwritten wisdom that in some families has become an honored tradition.

How to Read Your Tea Leaves

Before you begin, let go of any pressure to give specific predictions or answers for yourself or others. Explore the patterns of the leaves at your leisure and see what takes shape; you don't need to see a unicorn in your cup for your reading to be magical—a few dots, lines, or curves can tell you much about present and future influences.

Choose a large white or light-colored teacup with a saucer. A bowl-shaped one is better than a straight-sided mug, as you'll be able to see the distribution of the leaves more easily. You'll need fresh, loose tea—traditional or herbal—or you can tear open a tea bag and use the contents, but ensure that the tea isn't dust-like and old. You'll be drinking the tea with some small leaves in it. It's fine to add milk; milk won't affect the reading.

Think about your question and make your tea in a pot, or put one teaspoon of tea in your teacup and add boiling water. Leave it to brew for 3 to 4 minutes to allow the leaves to settle on the bottom of the cup.

When you've poured your tea from the pot, or you're ready to drink your cup-made tea, stop and look at the surface of the liquid:

> *Bubbles on the surface at the side of the cup:* Future love.
> *Bubbles swirling in the center:* Money coming. The more bubbles, the more money.
> *A whole single tea leaf, floating:* A visitor; a stranger.

Drink your tea, leaving some liquid in the bottom. If you prefer, pour out some of the tea rather than drink it, so around two teaspoons of liquid are left. You'll need enough liquid in the cup to swill the residual leaves.

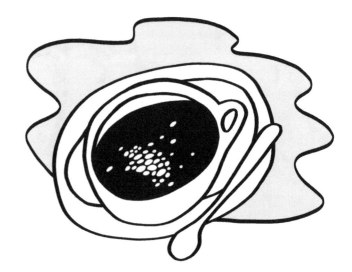

Next, hold the cup in your left hand and swill it counterclockwise three times, while thinking of your question or the life area you'd like to know about. Then slowly invert the cup on the saucer so the remaining liquid drains out. Leave the cup inverted for a minute or two. Then turn the cup the right way up and hold it in your right hand. You're ready to read the pattern of tea leaves inside it.

How to Interpret Your Cup

1. Begin by holding the cup with the handle toward you. See where the leaves are distributed; the area immediately below the handle represents you and your situation, so anything on the inside of the cup close to the handle is directly relevant to you. The region opposite the handle reveals what's away from you—people or events happening at a physical distance.

2. Examine the fall of the leaves. In folk tradition, evenly dispersed leaves were considered a good cup, while many leaves at the bottom of the cup were considered less fortunate.

3. Look at the leaf patterns. What marks and symbols do you see? Now turn the cup so you can see symbols from another angle. You may start with a bird and end with the initial M, for example. Take your time finding the symbols and let them evolve.

4. How large are the marks or symbols? The bigger the symbol and the clearer it is, the more important the event or influence.

5. Where do the symbols fall? The location of the symbols can modify their meaning. The rim and top areas of the cup traditionally denote happiness, whereas the bottom of the cup represents unhappy events. So if you were to get a good-fortune symbol near the rim, the symbol's location increases its positive message. A good-fortune symbol around the bottom of the cup dilutes some of the symbol's positivity. Likewise, a negative symbol around the top and rim means that the negative influence is short-lived.

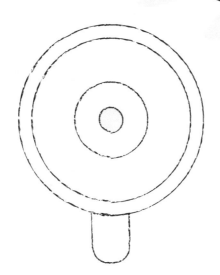

The location of events

Area opposite the handle:
People and issues at a distance

Handle:
Home, family, you

Tea Leaf Symbols

A

Acorn: Financial luck and good health.

Airplane: Unexpected travel; seeing from a higher perspective.

Anchor: Good luck and stability.

At the top of the cup: Good relationships and business achievement.

In the middle or bottom of the cup: A journey leading to money.

Angel: Love and good news; guidance and protection.

Ant: Strategy, hard work.

Apple: Discovery; the pursuit of knowledge; good health.

Arc: A need to get complete with a relationship or project that is currently on hold.

Arrow: Unwelcome news; criticism or aggression.

Pointing toward the cup handle: The aggression is directed at you.

Pointing away from the handle: You are the initiator.

Axe: Challenges.

B

Bag: Restriction. The need to think several steps ahead and expect underhandedness.

Ball: Going with flow; accepting ups and downs.

Balloon: Unexpected improvement.

Barrel: Focus on actions; time to move ahead rather than talk about it.

Bat: Choose your friends carefully.

Bear: Challenging territory ahead.

Facing away from the cup handle: A long journey.

Bed: Good organization and happiness.

Bee: Good news; hard work brings money and success; blessings.

Near the cup handle: Parties and happy gatherings.

Swarm of bees: Good fortune results from a group situation, such as a meeting.

Bell: A result or declaration. Look for other symbols nearby to see if this is favorable.

At the top of the cup: Promotion.

Two bells: A prosperous marriage; success.

Birds: Good news and journeys. See also *Raven*.

Boat: A short trip or help during stress; a place or time for recuperation.

At the bottom of the cup: If the boat is overturned, trust issues.

Book: Knowledge.

Open book: Education or a lawsuit.

Closed book: Spiritual development or hidden knowledge.

Boomerang: Karma. What goes around, comes around.

Boot: Good fortune and protection.

Bow: Hope and self-expression; expanding horizons.

Bracelet: Partnership.

Bridge: You find a fast route to success.

Broom: The way ahead is clear; minor irritations disappear.

Bull: Success in negotiations. Strength of character and good health.

Butterfly: Fun and socializing; charm and charisma.

Surrounded by dots: Money worries due to overspending.

C

Caduceus: Healing and money.

Near the cup handle: An important letter.

Cage: Restriction.

Cake: Celebrations, parties.

Camel: A responsibility; this may involve traveling.

Candle: Generosity and inspiring others.

Cart: Transactions: selling a house, receiving a legacy, or benefiting from a business deal.

Castle: A high position, but can warn against arrogance.

Cat: Hidden opposition. Someone may not be trustworthy.

Cell phone: Messages, news.

Circle or ring: Good fortune, love and commitment, success.

Broken by a line: Separation.

Chain: Established, successful relationships.

Broken: Breakup in a relationship or business agreement.

Chair: Stability; improvement at work.

Surrounded by dots: More money.

Chimney: Being of service to others.

Circle: Everything goes well; successful completion.

Claw: Protect your reputation and possessions.

Cloak: Lack of clarity. Delay any commitments, such as signing papers.

Clock: Do what you need to do now; don't procrastinate.

Clouds: Doubt and irritation, soon passing.

Clover leaf: Luck, particularly if a four-leaf clover.

At the top of the cup: Immediate success.

Coil: Confusion; the need to unravel a situation.

Coin: An agreement brings in money.

Column: High achievement.

Comma: Temporary rest.

Several commas: Procrastination.

Corn: Abundance.

Cow: Prosperity, growth, and happiness.

Cross: You may need to make a sacrifice to move on.

Crow: See *Raven*.

Crown: Trust and authority; being valued.

Cup: Rewards.

With dots around it: Financial reward.

D

Deer: Unexpected news. Other symbols close to the deer will offer further insights.

Dog: Faithful friendship.

At the bottom of the cup: A friend needs you.

Dot: Emphasizes the symbol next to it. See also *Butterfly, Chair, Cup, Knife, Letter.*

Dove: Harmony at home.

Dragon: A profound change that feels dangerous but is ultimately empowering.

Duck: Profit.

E

Eagle: Leadership and protection. Also a symbol of the father.

Ear: Keep your own counsel and ignore rumors.

Egg: Beginnings, creativity, fertility, and productivity.

Near the cup handle: A baby coming into the family.

Elephant: Wisdom and determination; patience and hard work bring success.

Eye: Insight and perception. You may need to supervise a situation closely.

Eyeglasses: An unexpected discovery.

F

Fairy: Romance and adventures; imagination and creativity.

Feather: Angelic guidance.

Fence: The need to set boundaries or feeling limited by them.

Fern: Uncertainty.

Fir tree: Success and influence.

Fire: Anger, outbursts.

Fish: Abundance, money, luck, and success.

Flower: A wish granted.

Fly: Temporary irritations; minor problems at home.

Fork: Decisions. Look for other symbols close by for guidance.

Fox: Betrayal and disloyalty; you may need to observe others closely and be vigilant.

Frog: A new home. Also, a need for humility.

G

Grapes: Abundance; indulgence.

Guitar: Love, attraction, and harmony.

H

Hammer: Focus; determination.

Hand: A new friendship and success.

Harp: Serenity, socializing, and new friends. In love, a happy partnership.

Heart: Love and happiness.

Two hearts close together: Commitment, such as marriage.

Hill: A test.

Horse: Serving others; loyalty and wisdom.

Horseshoe: Good luck; make the most of this opportunity.

House: Stability; good conditions for success at work.

At the top of the cup: Moving home.

Human figure: A visitor.

I

Insect: Worries. See also specific insects *Ant*, *Fly*.

Ivy: Reliable friends and support.

Near the cup handle: A faithful lover.

J

Jewel: A gift.

Jug: Generosity; supporting others.

K

Key: New opportunities; strategies for success; unlocking secrets.

Kite: Ambition; holding on to your goals.

Knife: Disagreement; separation.

Surrounded by dots: Arguments about money.

L

Ladder: Clear goals and commitment.

Lantern: The light within; inner knowing and protection.

Leaf: News.

> *If more than one leaf:* Happiness and success.

Letter: News. Look to see if there is an initial letter close to this symbol, as this can show who the letter, email, or text might be from.

> *If the letter symbol is surrounded by dots:* News about money.

Letters of the alphabet: Initials of a person or people.

Lily: Purity and integrity. Honest, clear communication.

Lines, crossed: Decisions to be made.

Lion: Honors and awards.

Lock: An obstacle; projects delayed.

Log: Stuckness; low energy.

M

Mermaid: Imagination, but also illusion and temptation. An offer may not be substantial.

Monkey: Mischief; playfulness.

Moon: A full moon means happiness and love coming.

> *If a crescent moon, waxing:* New projects and growth.

> *If a crescent moon, waning:* Decrease in interest; wait for a better time.

Mountain: Ambition and reward.

> *If the mountain has lines across it:* Challenges to be overcome.

Mouse: Lack of funds; the need to be more proactive.

Mushroom: Sudden growth or improvement.

> *Shown near a heart:* Romance; may need to take it slowly.

Musical note: Good luck.

N

Necklace: Love and relationships are important now. If the necklace is intact, love is stable; if broken, this suggests a breakup.

Net: Falling into a trap or netting a prize; proceed carefully.

Numbers: Gives a timescale (days, weeks, months).

O

Oak: Health and prosperity. Others rely on your strength.

Owl: Wisdom, but also caution; pay attention to detail.

P

Palm tree: Honors, success, and respect.

Pan: Self-containment; the need to break out of routines.

Parrot: Gossip.

Pear: Reward for hard work. Money flows; material comforts.

Pentagon: Good organization brings success.

Piano, piano keys: Peace and harmony.

Pig: Finding a balance between satisfaction and greed.

Pyramid: Past lives; origins and identity. Spiritual development.

Q

Question mark: You question your abilities or your intuition. A decision needs to be made.

R

Rabbit: Sensitivity and fertility; escaping problems that need to be addressed.

Rainbow: Hope and optimism.

Rat: Survival. You may need to act out of character to outwit an opponent.

Raven or crow: The need to find your life purpose; feeling unsettled and seeking stability.

Reptile: Intense emotions such as anger, guilt, or envy.

Ring: Completion, love, and friendship.

Road: The unknown future. New opportunities.

Rose: Affection, friendship, joy, and success.

S

Scales: Justice and decisions.

If the scales are balanced: You will be treated fairly.

If the scales are unbalanced: A decision goes against you.

Scissors: Misunderstandings and arguments.

Scythe: Sudden endings that are unavoidable. Seeing the truth.

Shark: Opposition. The need to show your strength.

Sheep: A wake-up call to speak up rather than follow a group consensus.

Shell: Inner wisdom and guidance.

Ship: A well-defined ship brings prosperity and health; if broken and ill-formed, disappointment.

If there are two or more ships: A successful commercial venture. See also *Boat*.

Snail: A slow, steady approach; this may be comfortable but not bring you timely results.

Snake: Wisdom and renewal, or mistrust; look at the surrounding symbols for further guidance.

Spade: Success comes from hard, consistent work.

Spider: Inventiveness, but the danger of overcomplicating what could be a simpler task; networks, news, and communication.

Spiral: A slow but steady rise to fame.

Spoon: A christening.

If two spoons: A fun flirtation.

Square: Restriction or protection. Look to the surrounding symbols for further guidance.

Stairs: Improvement; spiritual development.

Star: Happiness and good fortune; wishes come true.

Sun: Empowerment and happiness. Others are drawn to you.

Swan: Advancement.

If flying: Money coming.

Sword: Opposition and challenges to your position.

T

Table: Eating and socializing.

Teapot: Meetings and discussions; being asked for input.

Telescope: Foresight: seeing beyond the present.

Tiger: Prosperity; fierce attraction in relationships; aggressive tactics.

Tortoise: Slow progress and slow success.

Tower: The past; a discovery connected with the past shines a new light on the present.

Train: Expanding horizons. Events speed up.

Trees: Strength and growth, shelter and care; the family. See also *Oak*.

Triangle: Success.

Downward-pointing: Disappointment.

Trowel: Patient attention to detail now assures future success.

U

Umbrella: Protection.

Unicorn: Spiritual connection; imagination, art, magic, and creativity.

V

Vase: Being of service to others; sharing your gifts.

Violin: Following your own path; independence.

Volcano: Suppressed emotion.

W

Wasp: Being stung; hurtful actions or comments.

Web: Intrigue; being caught up in an unexpected situation; take good advice.

Whale: The ability to make a success of a great project.

Wheel: Change and progress.

Wing: Messages. See also *Angel*.

Wolf: Instinct. The need to fight for or protect others.

Z

Zebra: A nomadic lifestyle or a trip overseas; a secret affair.

CHAPTER

Palmistry

Palmistry may seem complex; there are many lines, marks, and symbols on the hand, and professional palmists spend years studying their meanings. However, much can be gleaned from just a couple features. A basic understanding, coupled with your intuition, will help you begin reading sooner than you thought possible.

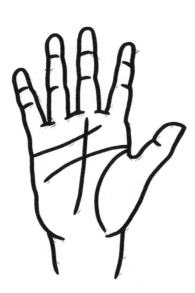

Learning to Read the Hand and the Palm

Palmistry has two aspects: chirognomy and chiromancy. *Chirognomy* means reading the shape and qualities of the hand (for example, gaps between fingers, the skin's texture, and joints). *Chiromancy* is the interpretation of the lines and other markings. Begin with chirognomy and practice reading on yourself and others.

One of the reasons palmistry is appealing is its ability to show timings, because all the major lines are divided into time segments. Palmistry also has much to say about health. However, our role as would-be palmists is not to diagnose or predict health issues; seeing one in the future does not mean it is unavoidable.

HOW THE LINES CHANGE OVER TIME

The lines on the palm can change over a two- to three-month period. If you regularly take palm prints (see page 75), you're potentially able to see how. A reading can also help pinpoint opportunities or danger points in the future. Armed with this knowledge, the person has a choice— to keep going along the same track or make decisions that will create an alternative outcome.

Left- and Right-Hand Meanings

If you are right-handed, your right, or active, hand shows how you're using your abilities; the left, or passive, hand shows the abilities you were born with. If you are left-handed, the reverse is true. For the purposes of this chapter, I refer to the right hand as dominant.

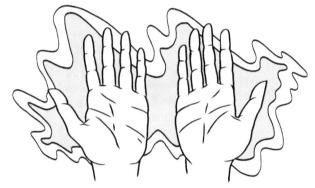

Left (passive) hand: Reveals inherited traits; early and family influences; your destiny.

Right (active) hand: Reveals if you are using or overlooking your natural abilities.

Note how the lines on the hand can differ; there can also be differences in the size of the fingers and mounts (see pages 68–71).

A palmist looks at both the left and right hands, but focuses mainly on the right hand during the reading, because this hand tells you what you are manifesting, and have manifested, now. He or she may refer to the left hand to see if you were born with a particular character trait or talent, and by comparing features and markings on the two hands can see if this is something you've developed. Comparing both hands is important, as it also reveals your future potential. For example, the palmist might see a well-developed mount of Mercury until the little finger of your left hand, and a flattish corresponding mount on your right hand. This shows that you have a natural ability to write and communicate that you're not yet using— an observation that offers a deeper realization of your special abilities.

Chirognomy

Chirognomy refers to the shape and qualities of the hand—the shape of the palm, fingers, and thumbs; fingertip markings and nail shape; finger gaps; the prominence of joints; and the skin's texture, for example.

Hand Position, Texture, and Color

First, look at the natural hand position. Try it on your own hand:

1. Turn your hand palm upward and rest your hand comfortably on a flat surface. Find a position that feels natural.

2. If your thumb is away from your hand and does not touch any of your fingers, you have an open hand. (It's likely that all or some of the fingers will be open, too.) This reveals an open character; you're open to ideas and opportunities, are willing to take some risks, and tend to be generous. If your thumb rests against or touches one of your fingers, this denotes a closed hand; you have a more cautious attitude to money and risk-taking, along with a need for privacy and discernment.

3. Now, look at the angle the thumb makes with the side of the hand:
   - **Less than 45 degrees from the side of the hand:** Closed, conservative nature.
   - **45 to 90 degrees:** Average—a balanced, open nature.
   - **More than 90 degrees:** Leadership qualities, but can be impetuous and headstrong.

An open hand has the thumb at an angle to the index finger.

A closed hand has the thumb touching one of the fingers.

Hand Shapes

Modern palmistry links hand shape to Earth, Air, Fire, or Water, an idea proposed by the British palmist Fred Gettings in *The Book of the Hand* (1965). If you have a mix of hand types, read the interpretations for both descriptions.

EARTH HAND

Qualities: Square palm; short fingers; clear, strong major lines on the palm.

They are: Fixers—reliable, pragmatic, direct.

They need: Routine, security, order.

AIR HAND

Qualities: Square palms; long fingers; clear, thin major lines on the palm.

They are: Communicators—talkative, analytical, cerebral.

They need: Emotional balance; ways to safely express feelings.

FIRE HAND

Qualities: Rectangular palms; short fingers; clear major and minor lines on the palm.

They are: Adventurers—energetic, sociable, passionate.

They need: To conserve energy by saying no on occasion, to release excess energy through exercise.

WATER HAND

Qualities: Rectangular palms; long fingers; thin major lines and lots of fine lines on the palm.

They are: Intuitives—emotional, sensitive, imaginative.

They need: Peace, time out, grounding through doing practical tasks.

Interpreting Finger Lengths

To interpret finger lengths, examine the fingers in terms of their relative proportions. For example, your little finger is considered long if the tip extends beyond the upper joint of your ring finger (even if all your fingers appear small and short). When you've noted this, the interpretations for the fingers that follow will make much more sense; you'll be able to choose the interpretations that best reveal particular aspects of your life.

Look at your finger lengths from the palm side, rather than the back of your hand, and cup your palm to get the straightest line where the fingers join the palm. As most people's palms are curved, this allows you to see the relative finger lengths more accurately than looking at a flat palm. Try it: Stretch out your palm and look at the relative lengths of your fingers. Now cup your palm so the bases of the fingers align, and the relative lengths will shift—particularly if you have a very curved palm.

With your fingers together, cup your hand to make a straight line across the base of the fingers, then look at the relative finger lengths from this position. Determine if your relative finger lengths are longer, shorter, or roughly equal to these average lengths:

Index finger: Stops halfway up the top phalange of the middle finger.

Middle finger: The finger is about the same length as the back of the hand (measuring from the knuckle to the wrist bone) or three-quarters of the length of the palm. Check this by placing the middle finger of one hand on the palm of the other hand, lining up the base of the finger with the base of the wrist.

Ring finger: Stops halfway up the top phalange of the middle finger.

Little finger: Reaches the top joint of the ring finger.

Thumb: To see your relative thumb length, hold the thumb in against the side of the palm. An average length thumb stops halfway up the base phalange of the index finger.

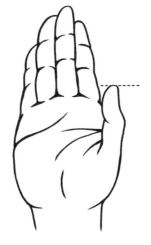

This thumb is considered short, as it stops before the halfway point on the index finger.

Fingertip Markings

To see the features on your fingertips, you may need to use a magnifying glass or take fingerprints. Note the fingers on which you have arches, whorls, and loops, then use the finger meaning to give an interpretation. For example, a whorl on the index (Jupiter) finger combines the whorl meaning (individuality) with the Jupiter meaning of ambition, so this would indicate you have a unique talent or skill you use in your professional and/or creative life.

- **Arches:** Practical and methodical; often clever with the hands. The need for security and routine.

- **Whorls:** Individuality; someone who has a special talent or skill.

- **Loops:** Sociable, communicative; a connector.

An arched fingerprint has a wave-like pattern.

A whorl is a spiral with lines curling around it.

A loop has radiating lines.

The Three Zones of the Palm

Look at the shape of the hand to see what motivates you most: ideas, intellect, and spirituality; practical achievements; or the material world of money, security, and sex. The whole hand can be divided into three zones, as follows:

- **Fingers:** The mental and intuitive zone: intellect, spirituality, brain power.

- **Middle of palm, including outer and inner Mars:** The practical zone: self-management, work-life balance, practical tasks.

- **Lower palm, including the thumb:** The material zone: money, security, drives and instincts, sex.

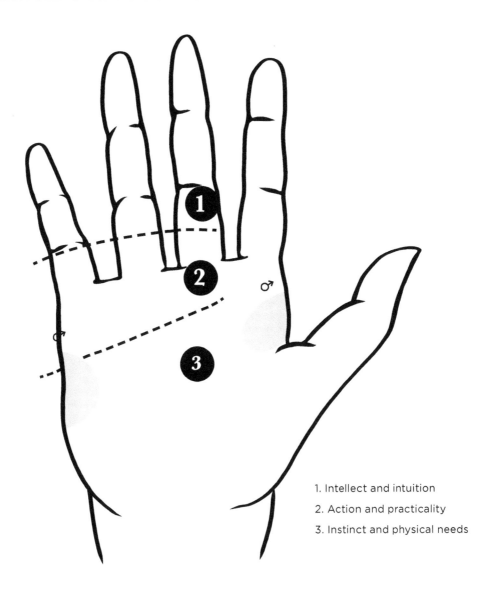

1. Intellect and intuition
2. Action and practicality
3. Instinct and physical needs

See which part of the hand is most prominent. What is your first impression—are your fingers long, or maybe the lower side of your hand is large and fleshy? Proportionally large fingers show an emphasis on the mental world, so you may spend a lot of time in your head. If the lower palm is prominent, then you're driven more by material and instinctual needs, such as sex, money, and security.

The Mounts of the Hand

There are seven primary mounts and one plain on the hands. Read the mounts for instant insight into a person's character. When you start to read the lines on the palm, knowing the meaning of the mounts helps you effectively interpret them.

The names of the mounts under the fingers are also given to that finger, so, for example, the Mount of Apollo is under the index, or Apollo, finger. The planet Mars, for aggression and energy, appears three times—as the inner mount of Mars, the outer mount of Mars, and the plain of Mars in the center of the palm. We also have Venus, under the thumb, and the mount of the Moon, opposite the Venus mount.

Slightly cup the palm to see the mounts. The higher, or more developed, the mount, the more of the qualities of that mount you have. Overall, the ideal palm has equally well-developed mounts. Mounts can be:

- **Flat:** Flat, thin, unremarkable.

- **Well-developed:** Risen, but not excessively.

- **Overdeveloped:** Overdeveloped, fleshy, prominent.

You can combine finger-length readings (see page 72) with mount readings. For example, if you have a short index (Apollo) finger and a flat mount of Apollo beneath it, this could show great dips in self-confidence, as low self-confidence is reflected in both the short index finger and flat mount. If you have an average-length index finger and flat Apollo mount, this would give the meaning that you're mostly balanced in your outlook but can lack confidence at times. It's easy to remember as follows:

- A long finger above a mount increases the attributes of that mount.

- A short finger above a mount reduces the attributes of that mount.

- An average-length finger above a mount adds balance.

Take note of your palm's mounts, then look up the interpretations below. Also, look to the lines of the palm for more information (see pages 75–91), as this can balance out flat mounts and show excessive qualities, too. For example, you might have doubts about a person with an overdeveloped mount of Mercury because they might exaggerate a little to please people, but if they have a well-defined head line, which shows trust, then you can rely upon them to tell the truth. If the mount of Jupiter is well developed, meaning a love of learning and an enterprising nature, look at the head line for confirmation. A well-marked head line supports this meaning, whereas a weak head line exaggerates the meaning and suggests egotism.

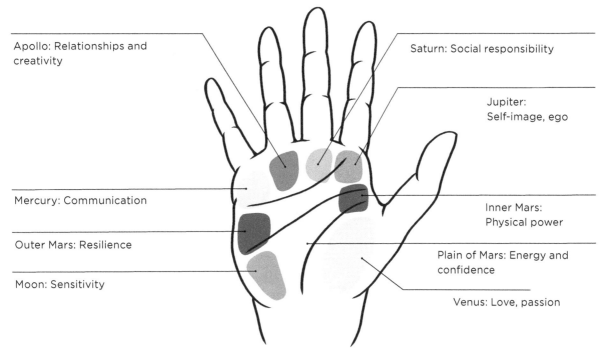

Apollo: Relationships and creativity

Saturn: Social responsibility

Jupiter: Self-image, ego

Mercury: Communication

Inner Mars: Physical power

Outer Mars: Resilience

Plain of Mars: Energy and confidence

Moon: Sensitivity

Venus: Love, passion

MOUNT OF MERCURY

Mercury qualities: Self-expression, communicating ideas.

Well-developed: Natural connector, honesty, commercial acumen.

Overdeveloped: Keen to please, so may omit difficult truths. If the little (Mercury) finger

is crooked, dishonesty and misinformation.

Flat: Poor communication skills, shyness.

MOUNT OF APOLLO

Apollo qualities: Creativity, sociability, emotions, the subconscious.

Well-developed: Artistic tendencies, charismatic, optimistic, versatile.

Overdeveloped: Attention-seeking, insensitive.

Flat: Focused outlook, limited interests beyond everyday affairs.

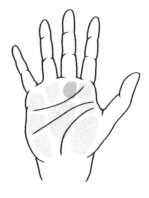

MOUNT OF SATURN

It is rare to have a developed mount of Saturn; on many hands it is not well defined, so as an alternative, read the interpretations for the middle finger (see page 72).

Saturn qualities: Responsibility, morality, seriousness.

Well-developed: Conservative, practical, reliable, cautious, studious.

Overdeveloped: Philosophical, serious, can be the gloomy martyr.

Flat: Wants to be cared for, can shirk responsibility.

MOUNT OF JUPITER

Jupiter qualities: Ambition, success, self-confidence, leadership, pride, ego.

Well-developed: Enterprising, focused; loves to learn.

Overdeveloped: Domineering, unreasonable, opinionated.

Flat: Can lack confidence, prefers direction from others.

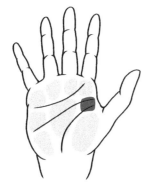

MOUNT OF MARS (INNER)

Inner Mars qualities: Physical power, self-esteem, physical courage, energy.

Well-developed: Well balanced and honest, will take determined action if necessary.

Overdeveloped: Aggressive, impulsive, could show anger physically.

Flat: Low self-esteem, insecurity.

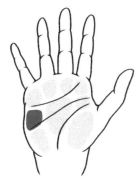

MOUNT OF MARS (OUTER)

Outer Mars qualities: Resilience, willpower, inner strength, moral courage.

Well-developed: Good self-control, takes appropriate action, loyal.

Overdeveloped: Impetuousness, irrationality, pomposity.

Flat: Overly passive, avoids confrontation, difficulty making commitments.

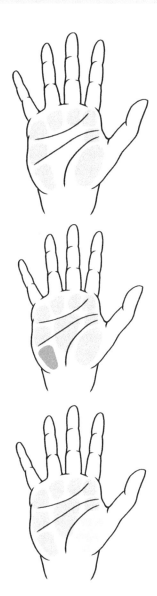

PLAIN OF MARS

Assess the plain of Mars by touching it.

Plain of Mars qualities: Confidence, energy.

Deep and firm: Balanced, secure, practical, confident. A hard feel can show lack of tact.

Soft and fleshy: Lack of motivation.

Soft and thin: A giver, can give too much energy to others, may lack confidence.

MOUNT OF THE MOON

Moon qualities: Sensitivity, creativity, imagination, intuition.

Well-developed: Artistic sense, compassionate, intuitive, receptive.

Overdeveloped: Imaginative, fantastical, ungrounded.

Flat: Skepticism, tactlessness.

MOUNT OF VENUS

Venus qualities: Love, emotion, passion, beauty, vitality.

Well-developed: Good relationships, happiness, energy

Overdeveloped: High libido, impetuousness, pleasure-seeking.

Flat: Low sex drive, lack of motivation, difficulty connecting with others.

Merged Mounts

Sometimes a mount may appear flat, but it has merged with the mount next to it. Merged mounts have interpretations based on the two mounts:

- **Jupiter and Saturn merged (beneath the index finger and middle finger):**
  Competitive, enterprising, practical ambition

- **Apollo and Saturn merged (beneath the ring finger and middle finger):**
  Can put ideas into practice; creative and practical

- **Mercury and Apollo merged (beneath the little finger and ring finger):**
  A career in writing and communication

Finger- and Thumb-Length Meanings

The fingers and thumb each link with an aspect of the self. Overall, the longer the finger or thumb, the stronger the attributes. Short fingers or thumbs diminish the attribute, as follows.

AVERAGE	SHORT	LONG
Index Finger: Ambition, leadership, self-confidence		
Well-balanced; realistic self-image	Lacking confidence	Strong; can be driven; if very long, intolerant
Middle finger: Resilience, morality, responsibility		
Good work-life balance	Uncertain, fears pressure	Overgiving, dependable
Ring finger: Creativity, emotions, the subconscious		
Articulate, sociable, open	Lower energy; cautious	Emotional, passionate, entrepreneurial
Little finger: Communication		
Balanced; good listener	Shy; difficulty communicating	Charismatic, talkative, good with words; can be impetuous
Thumb: Ego and willpower		
Reasonable drive	Team player; may lack motivation	Natural leader; could be domineering

Interpreting the Phalanges

Hold up your hand and look at the relative lengths of the phalanges on each finger. Are they even, or is one shorter or longer?

A quick way to read your phalanges is via the division of the top, middle, and lower into three categories (these categories also correspond to the three zones of the palm). The length of a phalange reveals how you think and act: long top phalanges (1) show you operate intuitively and focus on thinking; longer middle phalanges (2) show you're concerned more with action and practical tasks; and longer lower phalanges (3) denote that you're more concerned with the material world: money, security, and physical needs.

The fleshiness of a phalange also reveals an emphasis on these three categories. If your base phalanges, for example, are long and fleshy, this shows that having money and holding on to it is a key priority for you.

The thumb represents strength of character, and it's divided into two phalanges. The top phalange rules willpower and ability, while the lower phalange rules logic and reason. Look at the proportion of the phalanges—are they equal in length? Is one phalange fleshier than the other? If the top phalange is dominant in length and shape, this may show that your ambition sometimes overrides practicalities. If the lower phalange is larger or longer than the top phalange, you put practical considerations first rather than let ambition rule. The thumb is also an indicator of temper. A bulbous and/or red top phalange can show a fiery nature. If the thumb is broad and square at the tip and the top of the thumb is fleshy and rounded, this denotes anger and passion, but also insensitivity.

1. Intellect and intuition

2. Action and practicality

3. Instinct and physical needs

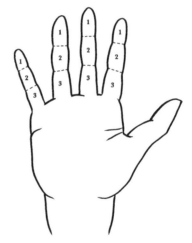

Interpreting Gaps and Leaning Fingers

Hold the back of your hand to the light or a light background, resting your elbow on a surface so you can see the natural position of your fingers. You may see that some fingers have prominent gaps between them, or they might naturally lean closer to other fingers.

Index Finger

Gap between index finger and middle finger: Good time management.

Index finger leans toward middle finger: Needs security, money is important, cautious.

Middle Finger

Gap between the middle finger and index finger: Good time management.

Gap between the middle finger and ring finger: Spontaneity, lives for the day, not a planner, can be erratic with money.

Middle finger leans toward the index finger: Needs more confidence.

Middle finger leans toward the ring finger: Family commitments, lots of responsibility, would like to take life less seriously.

Ring Finger

Gap between the ring finger and the middle finger: Spontaneity, lives for the day, not a planner, can be erratic with money.

Gap between the ring finger and the little finger: Someone who's a bit distanced from the rest of the world.

Ring finger leans toward middle finger: Someone who wants to be more responsible.

Ring finger leans toward little finger: Flair for words.

Little Finger

Gap between little finger and ring finger: A dreamer, prefers the spiritual to the material world.

Little finger leans toward ring finger: Prone to exaggeration, emotionally driven.

Crooked little finger: Someone who is not straight with the facts, who embroiders the truth or lies.

Chiromancy

Taken with what we know about the hand's shape, the lines on the palms help us build a bigger picture of a person's life.

Major Lines

The four major lines are the life line, head line, heart line, and fate line. They denote life events, how you think, your relationships, and your career path. As with chirognomy, remember to refer to the left hand as well as the right during a reading, so you can see how a person has developed (or has not been aware of) certain talents and abilities.

The Major and Minor Lines of the Hand

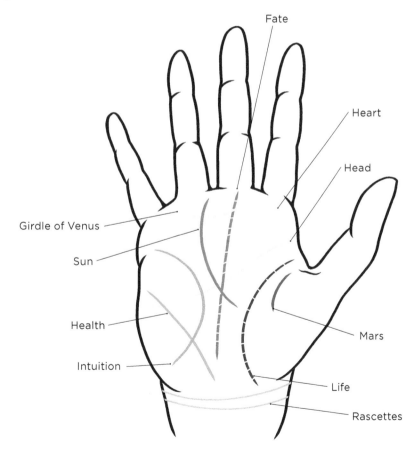

Fate

Heart

Head

Girdle of Venus

Sun

Health

Intuition

Mars

Life

Rascettes

Timing and the Major Lines

The four major lines are divided into years. The timing begins where the lines begin on the hand, so remember to read the lines from their starting points. An average life span of seventy-five years is used, but you will need to revise this if you are reading for a person older than seventy-five.

To begin, you may like to see how your line timings relate to events in the past, then look beyond your current age to see what may potentially happen in the future. As you have free will, these show likely events based on current circumstances.

Minor Lines

The minor lines include the Sun line, girdle of Venus, line of intuition, health line, marriage lines, line of Mars, children lines, and rascettes. You may have none or some of these lines, and some may be faint. If any lines are faint or absent, it does not have a negative connotation—in fact, a missing health line, for example, is seen as a positive sign (see page 86). Consider the minor lines as a source of additional or supporting evidence of what you have already gleaned from examining the hand and the major lines.

Timing and Major Lines of the Hand

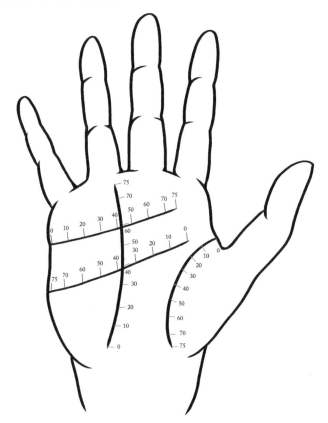

Major Lines

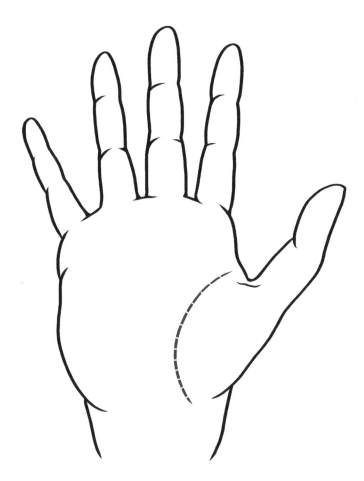

THE LIFE LINE: *Health and Vitality*

The life line on the left hand: Inherited traits.

The life line on the right hand: How you have dealt with inherited traits.

Description and location: The line that encircles the thumb. It begins above the thumb and ends toward the base of the palm (see page 75).

Length of the life line: The length of the line doesn't denote how many years you will live. It divides into five-year periods, so to see timings, work with the length of the life line you have. Most palmistry diagrams show seventy-five years as an average.

How it is marked: A clearly marked life line means strength, energy, and good health. A stronger life line on the left hand shows living more according to destiny; if the line is stronger on the right hand, this indicates greater self-confidence. A weaker life line means less energy and more susceptibility to illness (see also "The Health Line," page 86, which can suggest a stronger or weaker constitution).

A life line made up of lots of short, unconnected lines can show oversensitivity and nervousness, but also potential artistic brilliance. Noticeable gaps in the life line, such as islands, chains, and other markings, can show illnesses, stress, or other disruptions. Rays, or horizontal lines, coming from the mount of Venus across the life line represent troubles and challenges.

Other features:

- **Guardian angel lines:** These lines begin on the life line and extend downward. It's believed that they represent relatives or close friends lost at a specific age.

- **Rising lines:** if there are lines rising from the life line, see where they end, as this shows your efforts to achieve success in a particular area. For example, a rising line that finishes on the mount of Saturn, below the middle finger, shows a striving toward greater social responsibility.

- **Double life line:** This is a fainter line that runs alongside the life line and shows protection from life's difficulties. Some palmists also read the double line as a sign of prosperity and happiness.

The curve of the life line: The bigger the curve, the more generous the person is, and the more energy they have for other people. A slight curve or virtually straight life line running across the mount of Venus suggests a focus on the self.

The angle of the life line and head line: Cup your hand a little to see if the life line touches the head line. If it touches, this means prosperity. If the lines do not touch, look at the angle they make. The sharper the angle, the greater the luck.

Look on both hands for this: Some people have a life and head line that are apart on their left hand but have a touching life and head line on their right hand, showing that they have taken their destiny into their own hands, perhaps maximizing opportunities for wealth or becoming otherwise connected to it, such as through family or a partner.

You can also look at the point at which the head line and life line separate, as this reveals the age at which you gained independence as an adult.

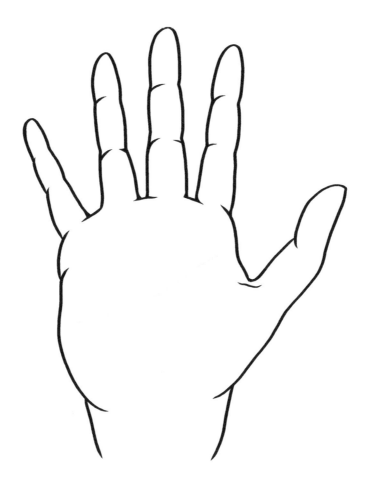

THE HEAD LINE: *How You Think*

The head line on the left hand: The intelligence you were born with.

The head line on the right hand: How you have developed your thinking.

Description and location: A horizontal line beginning on the thumb side of the palm that is above, crossing, or touching the life line. Note where the head line begins and where it ends, as these locations have meanings.

Length of the head line: A long head line can be a sign of high intelligence and a philosophical outlook; however, this person may use this ability to further their interests rather than directly helping others. A short head line shows a focus more on practical, immediate issues and could show that you are focused on a particular life area. Look on the palm to see where the head line begins and ends, as it has one of the following meanings:

- **Beginning on the mount of Jupiter, under the index finger:** Confidence and ambition

- **Beginning below the life line, so it crosses the life line:** Lack of confidence; risk-averse

- **Ending toward or on the mount of the Moon:** Imagination and mysticism, artistic ability

- **Ending toward or on the mount of Mercury, below the little finger:** Business or scientific leanings

- **Ending toward or on the mount of Saturn, under the middle finger:** Belief, philosophical thought, music

How it is marked: A strong, unbroken head line reveals good concentration, whereas a fainter line can show a lack of focus and possibly poor concentration. A broken head line may also be an indicator of headaches. Chains and breaks can mean obstacles and career challenges.

Other features:

- **The writer's fork:** A fork at the end of the head line on the mount of the Moon is known as the writer's fork because it denotes creativity in writing; it's a sign of literary talent.

- **A branch line from the head line to the heart line:** This denotes a love or fascination that may become obsessive. The heart rules the head—more so if a strong heart line lies close to the headline.

- **The angle of the head line and life line:** See "The angle of the life line and head line" on page 78.

The curve of the head line: A straight head line shows a logical approach to life, and that material things are important—less so the imagination. A downward-curving head line, ending on or near the mount of the Moon, reveals an intuitive disposition, and the greater the slope, the more intuitive and imaginative that person will be. A head line that is generally straight but curves upward toward the side of the palm on the upper mount of Mars shows business success—although this person could also be an unreasonable, demanding boss. A line that begins straight then curves downward shows a mix between the logical and the intuitive—a person who has the balance right.

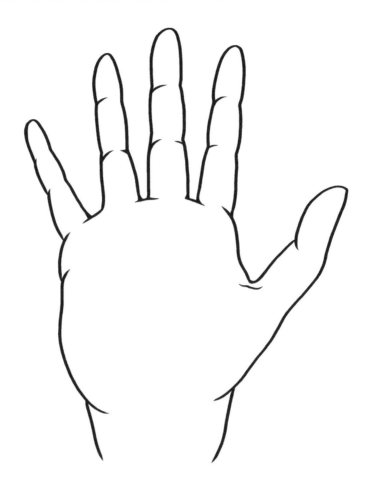

THE HEART LINE: *Emotions and Relationships*

Also known as: The mensal line or love line.

The heart line on the left hand: Your potential to love and to sustain relationships.

The heart line on the right hand: How you have developed that potential.

Description and location: A horizontal line running across the palm, above the head line. The heart line begins around the outer edge of the palm, under the mount of Mercury (at the base of the little finger).

Length of the heart line: A long line, extending right across the palm to the inner edge, shows a person who experiences strong or excessive emotions but can be so driven by their feelings that they entertain unreasonable jealousy and possessiveness. Shorter heart lines usually end on one of the following locations on the palm:

- **Under the mount of Jupiter, under the index finger:** This person is loyal and a romantic at heart but tends to idealize partners. For some palmists, this type of line-ending means fame to come.

- **Between the middle and index fingers:** This is a sign of a realist—loving, but down to earth.

- **The mount of Saturn, under the middle finger:** This is a passionate person who can be overly serious.

How it is marked: A strong heart line shows emotional security and stable relationships; a weak heart line shows emotional insecurity. Gaps in the heart line, lines of stress crossing it, and chains and islands can reveal relationship breakups and other emotional issues.

Other features:

- **A forked heart line:** When the heart line forks, with one line on the mount of Jupiter under the index finger and the other line between the index and middle fingers, this reveals happiness and affection in relationships.

- **The gap between the heart line and the head line:** The wider the gap, the greater the person's openness and generosity. So a narrow gap between the head line and heart line reveals a person who is more concerned with themselves than others. Another way of interpreting this narrow gap is to see which line is stronger. The stronger line means dominance, so a strong heart line close to the head line means the heart rules the head.

- **The curve of the heart line:** A curved heart line shows strong physical desire—and someone who tends to initiate sex. A straight heart line can show a person who is happy not to be the initiator; this person may also be romantic but is less sexually driven. If the heart line curves downward and crosses the head line and life line, it's believed to be a sign of past emotional trauma.

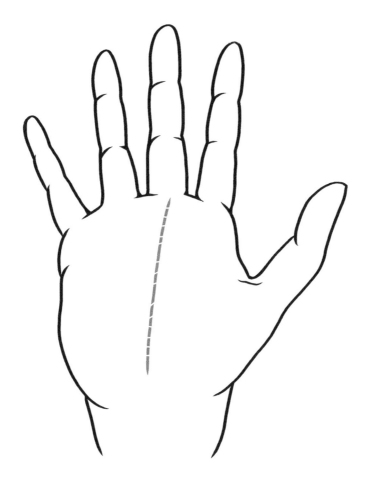

THE FATE LINE: *Career and Life Path*

Also known as: The line of destiny, line of fortune, line of Saturn.

The fate line on the left hand: Your career potential.

The fate line on the right hand: How you have developed that potential.

Description and location: A vertical line that starts toward the bottom of the hand and extends upward toward the middle, or Saturn, finger.

Length of the fate line: A long line, extending from the rascettes on the wrist or mount of the Moon to beyond the heart line shows personal drive and need to achieve; this person may have a creative vocation that stays with them for life. Look on the palm to see where the fate line begins and ends, as it shows at what life stage you have experienced, or can expect to achieve, success—and the kind of success that's available to you.

- **Beginning at the life line:** If strong, shows deserved success and merit. If low down on the life line, shows that early life may have been heavily influenced by the wishes of parents or other caregivers.

- **Beginning at the wrist, extends straight up to the mount of Saturn, under the middle finger:** Great success

- **Beginning on the mount of the Moon:** Success that is dependent on your reputation

- **Beginning on the head line and strongly marked:** Success comes later in life through hard work and talent

- **Beginning high in the plain of Mars (usually between the head line and heart line):** Difficulties—but if the line is strong afterward, shows difficulties overcome; the second half of life is often better than the first

- **Beginning on the heart line:** Success late in life after a difficult struggle

- **Ending on the mount of Jupiter, under the index finger:** Success and power. If the fate line has a branch going onto this mount, it shows early career success.

- **Ending on the mount of Apollo:** Success in the arts

- **Ending on the mount of Saturn:** See the interpretation for the long fate line, above.

- **Ending on the mount of Mercury:** Success in business and communications

- **Ending at the head line:** A mistake halts success; alternatively, this person may be dedicated to a profession until they are around forty, then choose another path (forty is the approximate age at which the fate line hits the head line).

- **Ending at the heart line:** Love gets in the way of success, or a person changes his direction to do something he loves, whether this is work-related or not; this is often shown by a new branch of the fate line rising from the heart line.

How it is marked: A strong, unbroken fate line shows a clear life and career direction, and that you feel in control of events and your life direction. A fainter line shows uncertainty in your career, and breaks literally show career breaks. If you see a fork, it shows having more than one interest or career; if there are little prongs with the fork, these show the number of new interests that call. If the forks develop into marked branches, see the areas of the palm where these branches end, as they show the life area that will capture this person's interest; the interpretations for these are as for the ending points listed above. For example, a branch running to the mount of Jupiter shows success early in that person's career.

Other features: A double or sister line next to the fate line shows two careers that you will follow.

Minor Lines

THE SUN LINE: *Success, Prosperity, and Creativity*

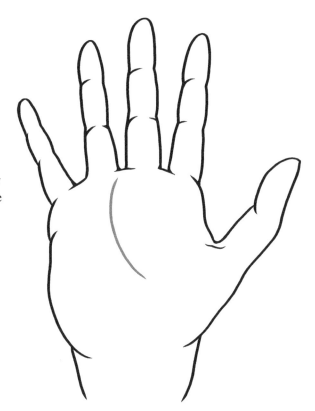

Also known as: The Apollo line, line of brilliance, line of success.

If absent, this is not a bad sign; look at the fate line for clues as to a person's success. If present, it enhances the positive attributes of the fate line (see page 100).

Description and location: A vertical line ending on the mount of Apollo (under the ring finger), it begins on or just above the wrist, on the mount of the Moon, or higher up on the hand. If you cannot find it, look first for a vertical line on the mount of Apollo and follow it downward.

Length of the fate line: Generally, the longer the line and the lower on the palm it begins, the greater the success potential. However, if it begins higher on the hand and is strongly defined, it can show prosperity later in life, after the person has found the right career path. The point at which the line begins is also associated with the following qualities and outcomes:

- **Beginning on the mount of the Moon:** Conditions that support success; success that comes from influential contacts.

- **Beginning on or near the life line:** Appreciation of the arts and love of beauty. If other signs on the hand are artistic—such as the writer's fork at the end of the head line (see page 80)—this reveals practical achievement in the arts.

- **Beginning on or near the head line:** The willpower to succeed.

- **Beginning on or near the heart line:** Following a goal close to your heart; passionate motivation.

- **Beginning on or near the fate line:** Great achievements.

Other features: A star on this line shows amazing success.

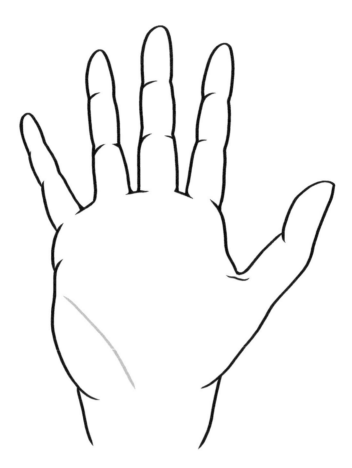

HEALTH LINE: *General Health and Stress*

Also known as: The Mercury, hepatic, or liver line.

If absent, this is a positive sign, generally meaning good health. If present, it can show whether someone is more resilient or vulnerable to stress and illness. A strong health line is more favorable than a weak line (see below).

Description and location: The line begins at the base of the palm, running almost diagonally over the palm to end below the mount of Mercury, under the little finger.

How it is marked: A strong health line indicates resilience to illness and stress, and the ability to manage energy levels well. A faint line with breaks can show a weak constitution, a tendency to worry about potential health issues, and potential illnesses. If there is a significant gap in the line, however, this is believed to show freedom from health problems during the gap period—you can time this from the illustration on page 76.

It is advisable to look at the life line (see page 77), which also indicates health, when reading the health line. Also, bear in mind that it is not appropriate to try to diagnose or predict health problems during a reading.

LINE OF INTUITION: *Clairvoyance*

Also known as: The psychic line, line of inspiration, bow of intuitions.

If present, the line shows psychic ability and strong intuition. If absent, you or the person you are reading for may still have psychic leanings—look for a long, pointed ring finger, a head line sloping downward onto the mount of the Moon, or the mystic cross marking (see page 91).

Description and location: A usually faint line forming a curve from the mount of the Moon to the mount of Mercury, under the little finger.

How it is marked: Even if faint, the presence of this line is still significant. It is believed that the stronger the line, the greater the psychic ability a person has. Examine the left hand to see if the line of intuition is present; if it is, you or the person you are reading for was born with this attribute. The right hand shows if this ability is being used.

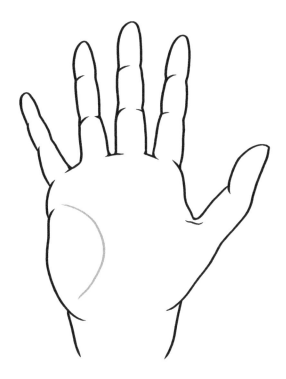

MARRIAGE LINES: *Significant Relationships*

Also known as: Relationship lines, lines of affection.

If present, these lines show significant love relationships, including marriage; there is one line for each relationship. If absent, you or the person you are reading for may have had relationships, but none yet of great significance. Look at the left hand to see if a marriage line, or lines, are present, as this shows the potential for these relationships in the future.

Description and location: Horizontal lines beginning on the side of the palm and extending to the mount of Mercury under the little finger (cupping the hand shows these lines, if present, more clearly).

How they are marked: The longer and deeper the line, the deeper the attachment.

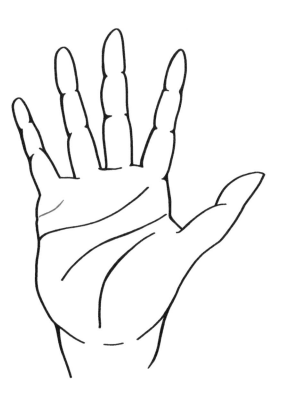

LINE OF MARS: *Extra Strength and Passion*

If present, the line of Mars denotes physical strength and strong drives. If absent, it does not mean you lack vitality and passion; you may have a line of Mars on your left hand or a strong life line (see page 77), which, if present, also indicates these qualities.

Description and location: A curved line within the life line on the mount of Venus; not to be confused with the double life line (see page 78), which runs close to the life line.

How it is marked: The stronger the line, the more powerful a person's strength and passion. The Mars line should also be interpreted with the life line, because it moderates or enhances its properties. If the life line is weak, with breaks showing potential illness or low energy, the line of Mars brings energy, so the outlook for that person would be more positive. If a Mars line appears with a strong life line, this can indicate intense passion and energy.

There is also a saying that if the line of Mars begins on the life line, this gives the age at which a love affair began or will begin.

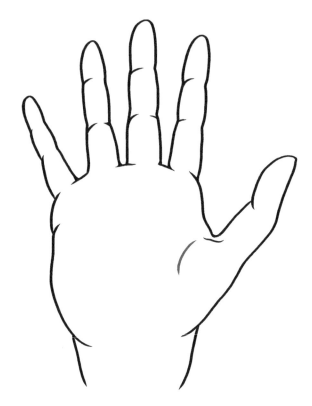

TIMING YOUR RELATIONSHIPS

You can use the marriage or relationship line(s) on your hand to see the ages at which you committed, or will commit, to relationships. Imagine that the area between the top of the heart line and the start of the little finger is divided into three sectors. Each one represents twenty-five years. The halfway point is thirty-seven years. So if you have a marriage line about halfway, this would show a major commitment at around the age of thirty-seven.

GIRDLE OF VENUS: *Passion and Sensitivity*

If present, this line denotes sensuality and passion, which may be expressed in relationships, a personal belief, or a dedicated cause. If absent, it does not mean that the person lacks passion or emotion; look at the mount of Venus and heart line (see page 81), for example, for an indication of emotions and sex drive.

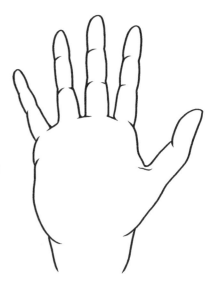

Description and location: A broken or unbroken semicircle that runs between the index and middle finger, and ring finger and little finger, over the mounts of Apollo and Saturn. The line can also extend to the edge of the palm, joining up with the marriage line (see page 87).

How it is marked: A faint girdle of Venus is considered better than a strong, unbroken marking, which indicates intense passion and emotion that may get in the way of decision making. A broken girdle is actually more positive, as it shows more emotional balance.

Length of the girdle of Venus: The girdle will usually end between the ring and little fingers but can end on the side of the palm, as below:

• Ending on the edge of the palm, joined to the marriage line: Very exacting standards in relationships.

• As above, but with breaks in the line: High expectations in love, but not unreasonably so.

RASCETTES: *Health and Travel*

Also known as: Bracelets of Neptune.

Description and location: One, two, or three lines running across the wrist. They are traditionally believed to be indicators of health.

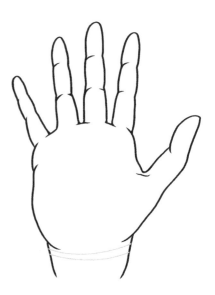

How they are marked: Bend your wrist slightly to see how the lines are marked. If clearly marked, they show good health. Two lines are considered ideal. But do refer primarily to the life line (page 77) and health line (page 86) if present, for health indicators. If the first line arches up onto the palm, this can be interpreted, in a woman's hand, as fertility problems. If the first line is chained or broken, this suggests a weak constitution and a need to take extra care of your health. If the lines below it are strong, this gives a more positive health interpretation.

Other features: Vertical lines running up from the rascettes to the mount of the Moon show the urge to travel.

Some palmists believe that rascettes are signs of good luck, so three rascettes would signify excellent fortune.

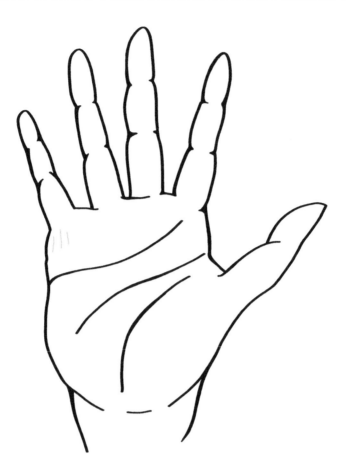

CHILDREN LINES

When present, these lines show the number of children you have or will potentially have including stepchildren, adopted children, and other children with whom you have a strong bond. On a male hand, children lines show he is fond of children; the number of children is believed to be shown on a female hand. If children lines are absent, this can show that a man or woman may not want to have children or is not ready. Check the mount of Venus: If it's flat, there is less inclination to have children; if it's fleshy, more so (and also an indicator of fertility). If there is a branch line running from the heart line up to the mount of Saturn, under the middle finger, this can also indicate the desire for children.

Description and location: Vertical lines that rise from marriage lines or appear close to them.

How they are marked: Children lines are usually more deeply marked on a woman's hand. Thick lines are believed to indicate boys, while thin lines show girls. A forked line shows twins. To count the number of children, count the lines from the outside of the palm.

Other Markings

Unless otherwise noted, see where these marks are located on the palm and relate them to the life area of the line or mount (see the illustration on page 75).

The Great Triangle: Health and Good Fortune

Formed by the intersections of the life line, head line, and health line. A large, well-marked triangle is a sign of good physical health, strong character, and luck.

Mystic Cross: Esoteric Adventures

A cross in the center of the palm, between the heart and head lines and the fate and Sun lines. (If you don't have a Sun line, look for an upright or diagonal cross in the center of your palm between the heart and head lines.) Signifies interest in the occult.

Triangle: Talent

Only read triangles marked with strong lines. Triangles mean talent and skill. On the mounts, they mean:

- **Mount of Jupiter:** Diplomacy.

- **Mount of Saturn:** Esoteric knowledge; clairvoyance.

- **Mount of Apollo:** Artistic ability.

- **Mount of Mercury:** Business acumen.

- **Mount of upper Mars:** Courage; martial strategy.

- **Mount of lower Mars:** Talent in science.

- **Mount of the Moon:** Ability to express imagination; travel.

- **Mount of Venus:** Great love.

Star: Shocks

Stars, made up of five or more legs, show shock events—for example, on the heart line it would indicate a breakup or revelation that leads to a fundamental change in that relationship. However, on the mount of Jupiter, a star denotes personal success.

Cross: Difficulties

Generally negative, a cross means stress, disappointment, or difficulties. The exceptions are the mystic cross and on the mount of Jupiter. Because Jupiter stands for ego and ambition, the cross indicates a break in this attitude, denoting love and affection.

Square: Protection

A sign of protection, it might surround a line or broken line or appear on a mount. It offsets any negatives in a line; time the appearance of the square, and you will see the time period of protection.

Grille: Interference

Grilles, grids of crossed lines, denote problems and obstacles. Unless the grille is on the mount of the Moon, and the Sun line is clearly marked, which means literary talent.

CHAPTER

Divination with Tarot Cards

Tarot is for insight, guidance, inspiration, self-understanding, healing, and prediction. Working with tarot is one of the greatest gifts you can give yourself, because the cards connect you with your inner guidance—and your own life story. There are myriad decks available, and it's important to choose a deck that calls to you. The tarot presented in these pages is the Universal Waite, which presents Pamela Colman Smith's drawings recolored by Mary Hanson-Roberts.

How the Deck Is Structured

The tarot deck comprises seventy-eight cards, divided into two groups, or *arcana* (arcana means "secret"). There are twenty-two major arcana cards, which can also be referred to as *trumps* or *keys*, and fifty-six minor arcana cards, arranged into four suits.

The twenty-two cards of the major arcana represent key turning points and decisions. If you're a beginner, it can help to interpret the major arcana cards in your spread first, then move to the minors, as you'll get the heart of the matter first. The majors are also a cycle, beginning with 0 The Fool, a beginning, and ending with XXI The World, or completion. The cards form a circle, known as the journey of The Fool, who travels through life physically and spiritually and is reborn with the World before he begins his journey again at zero. In this way, the numbers of the major arcana cards can show you where you are in any life phase. For example, cards with lower numbers, such as I or II, can give you the additional meaning of a new or young situation.

The fifty-six minor arcana cards are divided into four suits: Cups, Pentacles (or Coins), Wands (or Staves), and Swords. The suits may vary depending on your deck.

The Court cards are the Page, Knight, Queen, and King of each suit. They can be interpreted as people or as situations.

- **Pages** represent young people or young situations, such as an application for a new job or a budding new idea.

- **Knights** represent action. The Knights of Wands and Swords take fast action, the Knight of Cups is less forceful, and the Knight of Pentacles is slower and more considered in his approach.

- **Queens and Kings** represent achievement; a King and a Queen in the same spread can signify a couple, particularly if these cards fall close to each other.

How to Begin

Find a quiet space with a clean, flat surface. If you are working with a new deck, sort your cards into their arcanum and suits. If they come supplied in order, touch each card in turn as you look at each image. This creates a physical link with every card. Holding your cards, set an intention that you are energetically connected to them, and that your readings are for the highest good. If you prefer, you can make a fan of the cards and hold it to your heart (with the card backs on the outside of the fan), then set your intention.

Store your cards by wrapping them in a reading cloth—a piece of fabric you lay the cards on when you read. Don't allow other people to handle them casually.

Shuffling Your Question into the Cards

As you shuffle the deck, think of your question, imagining that your cards are absorbing the words. You can ask an open question such as, "What do I need to see/know today?" or make a request: "Tell me about X situation." Repeat your question out loud or in your mind as you shuffle; stop when you are ready.

If you're reading for someone else: Hand the deck to the person you are reading for—the questioner, or querent. Ask them to shuffle, thinking of their question or situation as they do so, then return the deck to you.

Choosing Cards for a Spread

There are three ways to do this:

1. Cutting the deck. Take the deck in your left hand and make three piles. Choose one pile, pick it up, and gather the remaining two piles under it, working from left to right.

    If you're reading for someone else: Ask them to make three piles with their left hand, choose a pile, then gather the remaining two piles under it as before. Take back the deck and hold it facedown, ready to deal the cards from the top of the pile.

2. Fanning the cards. Spread all the cards facedown in a fan shape and choose, with your left hand, the number of cards you'll need for your spread.

    If you're reading for someone else: Fan out the cards and ask them to choose the cards for the reading with their left hand, then pass each card to you in turn to lay out in your spread.

3. Any way you like. Choose your cards at random, plucking a card from any place in the deck.

Reversed Cards

Every card has an upright meaning and a reversed meaning. You can choose to read the reversed meanings of the cards, but many readers prefer to turn any reversed cards the right way up and read them all upright.

When you turn your cards faceup to begin a reading, turn them side to side, rather than flipping them upside down. Otherwise your upright cards will appear reversed, and vice versa, which affects their meaning.

A First Reading: Essential Techniques

For this reading, we ask "What do I need to see?" The cards will reveal the key influences around you now. Reading a small number of cards without laying them in a defined spread offers a way for you to interpret them freely. You'll get to see relationships between the majors and minors, and you'll notice patterns, such as cards with the same number or suit. These are the essential techniques of the professional reader. As you practice, you will find that your intuitive response to the cards steps in, and you do not need to consciously think about technique. These examples, therefore, are starting points, a way to activate your creativity and intuition in ways that will make your readings unique to you.

Choose four cards from the deck and shuffle them, making your request to see whatever is important now, then choose your cards: Cut the deck, lay the cards out in a fan shape, or choose any card from the deck at random. Place your four chosen cards facedown in a row. When you are ready to begin, turn over all the cards.

For example:

1. Look at the major arcana cards. We have one here, The World, so the focus is completion. This major card acts a theme for the reading—a project or goal is about to be achieved. Success and reward are coming.

2. Look at the minor arcana cards. Three suits are shown—Swords, Cups, and Pentacles—so it's likely that the completion The World brings will benefit other areas of your life. Pentacles show money, so you may be paid when you complete the work; Cups reveal emotions, so this project may be close to your heart and bring personal fulfillment; while Swords represent thoughts and the intellect, showing that finishing the work or achieving the goal is an expression of your ideas, and now that the work is almost done, you will free up some much-needed mental space.

3. Look at duplicates. There are two Queens. These can represent two aspects of yourself—the Cups, your feelings, and the Coins, the material, worldly aspect. You're in a powerful position financially and in a positive emotional space.

4. Look at the numbers on all four cards. In this example, note how The World's number, XXI, symbolizes the other cards. It has two tens, a repeat number, suggesting the repeat of the two Queens in the reading. The 1 of XXI gives us the Ace of Swords, beginnings. The World, the card of completion, also signifies new beginnings, so you can interpret the Ace as a new start or project that is coming. You might also see the Ace as guidance. To get to your goal, be decisive, put your feelings to one side, and find the most efficient way to tie up loose ends.

Past, Present, Future

This spread is a tarot classic, and it's one of the most direct methods for getting right to the heart of a question and seeing the potential outcome. You can use this spread to inquire about a specific situation—say, a project, relationship, or finances—or for general insight into the influences most affecting you now.

Shuffle your question or request into the cards, then choose three (from a fan, by cutting the deck, or choosing at random). Lay them out, facedown, in the following order. Turn them faceup one at a time, or turn them all faceup together—whatever feels right—and begin your interpretation (see the card meanings on pages 101–123).

1 PAST   2 PRESENT   3 FUTURE

The Celtic Cross

The Celtic Cross is the layout that professional readers turn to time and again. It gives more detail and context than the three-card reading, helping you see more aspects of your situation.

Shuffle and choose your cards, then lay the ten cards facedown. Turn over cards 1 to 6 and interpret them in turn, then turn over and interpret cards 7 through 10.

Card 1. Your current situation

Card 2. What is crossing or complementing you

Card 3. The best you can expect at present

Card 4. Hidden factors around you, or the "foundation," the real reason for the reading

Card 5. Past events influencing the present*

Card 6. Your next move*

Card 7. How you see yourself; what you can do

Card 8. Your environment; how others see you

Card 9. Hopes and fears

Card 10. The most likely outcome

*Some readers reverse positions 5 and 6. They lay the central cross, then one card above it and one below, but then lay a card to the right, then a card to the left. You can try the spread in the card order shown above, then try swapping cards 5 and 6 and see how this affects your reading. Go with whatever layout works best for you.

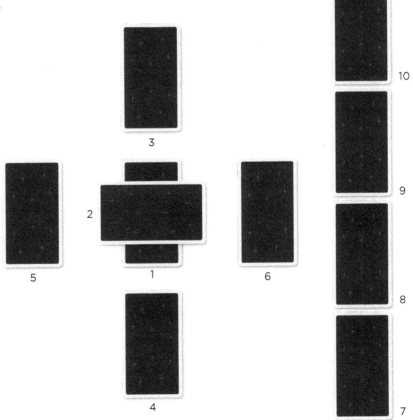

The Week Ahead

To look at the week ahead, shuffle and choose eight cards. First, lay down the Significator card facedown, followed by seven further cards in the order shown below. Keep the Significator facedown, but turn all the other cards faceup and interpret them. Finally, turn over the Significator; this gives you the overall theme of the week and helps you bring together the meanings of the other cards.

Significator: The general theme of the week

1 Monday
2 Wednesday
3 Friday
4 Sunday

5 Tuesday
6 Thursday
7 Saturday

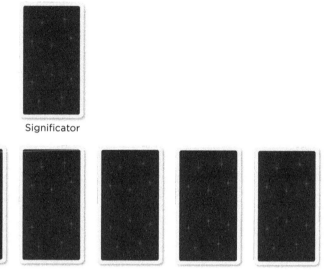

Significator

| 1 Mon | 5 Tue | 2 Wed | 6 Thur | 3 Fri | 7 Sat | 4 Sun |

Cleansing Your Deck Between Readings

Cards absorb the energies of their environment and hold the emotion of a reading. So before you read, you'll need to clear down your deck.

1. Go through the deck and turn any reversed the right way up.

2. Next, choose one or both of these instant cleansing techniques:

   • **Blowing:** Hold your deck in one hand and flick it as you blow across it.

   • **Knocking:** Hold the deck in one hand, with the cards facedown, and knock out unwanted energies with a firm, single knock on the top of the deck.

Card Meanings

The interpretations for the cards appear here, but also note your intuitive responses to your cards; it's worth taking a note of your own impressions first, before reading the traditional card meanings here, which are for guidance rather than rote learning. Work in a way that feels right for you.

The Major Arcana

0 THE FOOL

KEYWORDS: Innocence, risk, beginnings.

The Fool represents a major new life chapter. This is your call to adventure, to journey into unknown territory through physical travel, or a new career or spiritual path; this adventure is not without risk, however. The cliffs represent danger; the mountains, challenges; and the dog, barking a warning at our Fool, is a reminder to look before he leaps. The card can often appear in a reading after a relationship breakup as a sign of awakening to new possibilities ahead.

ADVICE: Embrace adventure but know the risks.

REVERSED MEANING: Idealistic thinking may cloud practical considerations. Foolishness.

THE FOOL.

I THE MAGICIAN

KEYWORDS: Action, willpower, success.

The Magician transforms thought into action through his will; he understands the flow of energy, symbolized by the figure eight or lemniscate, and works with it to create powerful change. The Magician calls you to create and communicate, and the card often heralds new projects, travel, and news. You have the resources you need to act, shown by the four minor arcana suit symbols on the Magician's table: Intelligence and reason (the Sword), heart (Cup), security and finance (Pentacle), and drive and passion (Wand).

ADVICE: Manifest your ideas now.

REVERSED MEANING: Deception; being charmed by an untrustworthy individual. Also, miscommunication and delays to plans.

THE MAGICIAN.

II THE HIGH PRIESTESS

KEYWORDS: Secrets, wisdom, the spiritual world.

The High Priestess is the clairvoyant, the translator between the realm of spirit and the earth plane. She asks you to connect with your intuition and to follow your spiritual calling. The card also denotes the need for privacy and keeping secrets and highlights the importance of the inner world and the power of unconscious knowing. The High Priestess as a keeper of wisdom arises too for learning and mentoring, and the teacher or spirit guide who connects with you when the time is right.

ADVICE: Value privacy and your spiritual practice.

REVERSED MEANING: Following a wrong path or breaking a confidence. A person who uses secret knowledge to gain power or status.

THE HIGH PRIESTESS.

III THE EMPRESS

KEYWORDS: Abundance, generosity, creativity.

The Empress brings abundance, so finances, relationships, and domestic projects thrive now. Harmony and balance benefit you, so this is a card of reassurance if you have been struggling financially or wondering if a relationship will grow. The Empress also denotes generosity and the ability to give and receive loving support. As the earth goddess, she connects us with the cycles of nature, family, and fertility. You may also seed ideas for new creative projects.

ADVICE: Nurture people and projects.

REVERSED MEANING: Financial challenges or fertility issues, creative blocks, or relationships out of balance.

THE EMPRESS.

IV THE EMPEROR

KEYWORDS: Control, security, order, authority, ambition.

The Emperor is the father or traditional male partner, a figure of authority and leadership. In a reading, he shows order is restored, and you are back in control of a situation. As the Emperor protects the boundaries of his territory, the card calls you to prioritize what is important to you and to take a methodical rather than intuitive approach; following due process gives the best results. As he represents authority, an additional meaning is taking on more responsibility and power; the card often arises in readings to show promotion.

ADVICE: Put practical matters first; get organized.

REVERSED MEANING: Feeling restricted by outdated attitudes or bullied by a domineering yet ineffectual individual.

THE EMPEROR.

V THE HIEROPHANT

KEYWORDS: Education, unity, spiritual direction.

The Hierophant denotes unity, but he holds many diverse meanings: education, orthodox beliefs, commitment, and public life. Overall, though, when he appears in a reading, you're about to move up a level; you honor your personal growth by being willing to learn and accept new responsibility, so you may embark on an educational course, take on a community role that may involve mediation, or decide to take a business or creative venture to new heights. Spiritually, the card shows self-connection, wisdom, and divine law. In relationships, the Hierophant brings a love commitment such as marriage.

ADVICE: Commit and learn.

REVERSED MEANING: The potential abuse of power, and unfair criticism.

THE HIEROPHANT.

VI THE LOVERS

KEYWORDS: Love and relationships, maturity, decisions.

The Lovers foretell an important decision. You may need to decide to stay part of a couple or be single; to choose between potential partners; or between lust or long-time love (a traditional association of the card is love triangles). Although the card highlights love and relationships, it has meaning in every reading. In work and business, for example, you may have the option of short-term contracts or permanent work. The best decision may not be the easiest, but the Lovers ask you to look beyond immediate gratification toward long-term happiness and fulfillment.

ADVICE: Take the path that supports your future growth.

REVERSED MEANING: Being let down in a relationship or taking the easiest, but not necessarily the best, option.

THE LOVERS.

VII THE CHARIOT

KEYWORDS: Determination, victory, a journey.

The Chariot shows you are moving into a success phase. The charioteer directs his sphinx-chariot by willpower rather than harness, so steady determination moves him forward; he cannot allow his ego to get out of control. The light and dark sphinxes symbolize the dark and light aspects of his personality and the stars symbolize cosmic protection. In a reading, the card says that if you take careful responsibility for your career and personal life, you will continue to progress and grow. It can also predict significant journeys, a new vehicle, new work and residences, and/or a commitment to be fully in a relationship—or alone.

ADVICE: Your determination brings success.

REVERSED MEANING: Arrogance and displays of ego, important details may be overlooked, journeys may be delayed.

THE CHARIOT.

VIII STRENGTH

KEYWORDS: Patience, tension, strength.

The maiden symbolizes the higher self and the lion symbolizes our baser instincts. Holding open the animal's jaws, she is peaceful and patient, holding her ground. The lemniscate signifies the flow of life and infinite possibility. In a reading, Strength says you may need your inner strength when dealing with conflict within yourself, or with an external challenge to your position. The need for compassion is an additional meaning, and Strength also appears in readings to show physical strength and recovery after illness or stress.

ADVICE: Call upon your inner strength.

REVERSED MEANING: Avoiding conflict rather than confronting a challenge.

STRENGTH.

IX THE HERMIT

KEYWORDS: Solitude, healing, contemplation.

The Hermit, guided only by the light of his lamp, travels alone in darkness. This is the card of contemplation and shows a time for solitude; this is a choice, rather than a situation to be endured, however. You may need time to write, study, meditate, or heal, or you may need peace and time away from pressure. You may feel called to reflect on a recent event and more deeply understand your role within it. The card often shows up after a relationship breakup or to illuminate a new educational or spiritual path.

ADVICE: Look within for the wisdom you seek.

REVERSED MEANING: Unwanted solitude. You may be feeling unsupported or rejected, but this situation can and will change.

THE HERMIT.

X THE WHEEL OF FORTUNE

KEYWORDS: Fate, improvement, intuition.

The Wheel represents Fate, the working of destiny in the world. As it turns, good fortune comes, so this is a card of hope and optimism. Problems are solved, and you move to a happier, productive phase. As the card is linked with fate, it suggests a connection with other realms and can show psychic ability, especially if it appears with card II, the High Priestess. The Wheel gives you the gift of luck and great potential for achievement.

ADVICE: Allow and appreciate destined gifts.

REVERSED MEANING: Even when reversed, the outlook is positive. A difficult phase is almost over; an upturn is coming.

WHEEL *of* FORTUNE.

XI JUSTICE

KEYWORDS: Balance, perception, objectivity.

The Justice card reveals being judged by others, rather than the self. In a reading, the card signifies the law profession, along with assessment and decisions in other life areas. And justice will be done, provided you are deserving and speak the truth. Past errors are put right, so if you have been mistreated, or your reputation damaged, the card is reassurance that the situation will be positively resolved. Life comes back into balance.

ADVICE: Stay true to your values.

REVERSED MEANING: There may be unfair treatment, discrimination, or a miscarriage of justice.

JUSTICE.

XII THE HANGED MAN

KEYWORDS: Waiting, sacrifice, enlightenment.

The Hanged Man is often linked with the Norse god Odin, who hung from the World Tree, after which he was given the gift of prophecy. His time of suspension between worlds—a shamanic initiation—was worthwhile because of the magical gift he received. In a reading, this card shows you in limbo, waiting for a decision, for events to unfold. Use this time to see your situation from another angle; there may be a higher purpose to this stasis, an insight that awaits you. The card can also show that you may need to make a sacrifice to move forward.

ADVICE: See your situation from another perspective.

REVERSED MEANING: Naïveté; making unnecessary sacrifices.

THE HANGED MAN.

XIII DEATH

KEYWORDS: Endings, release, transformation.

Death is not physical death, but a process of change through which our lives are transformed for the better. We may not welcome this skeletal figure with his scythe, but he is a representation of cycles of change that is necessary and absolute. It is time to accept what cannot be part of the future. In a reading, the card often arises to show the end of a relationship, job, or old situation. With Death comes truth—down to the bone, you now see what remains. Endings bring beginnings, so this card in your reading also signals new beginnings and growth.

ADVICE: Let go without fear.

REVERSED MEANING: Resistance to moving forward, holding on to the past.

DEATH.

XIV TEMPERANCE

KEYWORDS: Balance, reconciliation, healing, angelic guidance.

The Temperance angel pours water between two pitchers; the water flows in two directions, so we are witnessing a miracle. You may need a little divine intervention to deal with current pressures and demands, to find the right formula to keep everything flowing. Temperance signifies the need to carefully negotiate terms and often to mediate between difficult people. Relationships need emotional balance, and in financial affairs, the card often asks us to temper, or control, spending. Spiritually, Temperance suggests angelic guidance.

ADVICE: Get the balance right, and you can succeed.

REVERSED MEANING: Being a martyr to others' unreasonable demands, being emotionally overwhelmed; overspending and debt.

TEMPERANCE.

XV THE DEVIL

KEYWORDS: Enslavement, temptation, contracts.

The Devil symbolizes temptation and agreements that are, or have become, restrictive. These may be unhealthy contracts we have with ourselves, or other binds that enslave us. The card also reveals toxic relationships, lust, addiction issues, and negative thinking patterns—whatever seeks to control you. As the two figures on the card are not tightly chained, they can walk free whenever they choose. You, too, can free yourself from any negative situation more easily than you think.

ADVICE: You can be free now.

REVERSED MEANING: The restriction of the upright card may feel acute, but you can break the ties that do not serve you.

THE DEVIL.

XVI THE TOWER

KEYWORDS: Destruction, enlightenment.

The Tower signifies sudden destruction. In a flash, you see the truth of a situation; what you had thought was secure is subject to greater forces. There is no reason or blame for it. In this way, the Tower is a card of enlightenment and breakthrough, bringing release after an intense buildup. The card appears in readings to show the sudden ending of a relationship, issues with a house, or a huge knock to the ego. The impact may be shocking, but you are now able to rebuild.

ADVICE: Surrender and welcome the new.

REVERSED MEANING: The Tower may leave you reeling, but there is no need for bitterness or blame. It's time to recover.

THE TOWER.

XVII THE STAR

KEYWORDS: Hope, guidance, inspiration, creativity.

The Star maiden pours water from the pitcher of the past, to her left, and the pitcher of the present; the water symbolizes flowing thought and emotion. She nurtures the pool of life, guided by the star above her. The twilight denotes the magical time between night and day, signifying transition; changes are coming that will lead you closer to your higher purpose. In a reading, the Star also brings creative opportunities and divine guidance. The card is also associated with healing, as her watering gives nourishment and leads to growth.

ADVICE: Be hopeful and inspired.

REVERSED MEANING: When feeling unsupported, don't give up; follow the guiding light within.

THE STAR.

XVIII THE MOON

KEYWORDS: Illusion, dreams, crisis.

The Moon is the card of dreams, mystery, intuition, and doubt. In moonlight, nothing is as it seems, and the crayfish, symbol of the soul, must decide to go forward and escape the dog and wolf or stay safely in the water. The crayfish can signify a realization that is just under the surface of your conscious awareness, so this card is often a sign of disturbance—something important needs your attention. However, this is not a matter of applying logic. Your dreams and creative or spiritual practices may help you see what is at stake.

ADVICE: Let your intuition guide you toward a realization or decision.

REVERSED MEANING: Avoiding a deep or complex issue.

THE MOON.

XIX THE SUN

KEYWORDS: Success, protection, health, happiness.

The Sun is one of the most positive cards in the tarot deck, as it denotes happiness, achievement, and recuperation; stress dissolves as you enjoy simple pleasures, from spending time with family to enjoying restorative time alone—however you like to recharge. The sunflowers represent growth and health and the wall represents protection, so the Sun can also indicate recovery after illness and, more generally, vitality and reward. At a literal level, the card sees you on vacation away from home, or enjoying creative pursuits that nurture your inner child. The Sun overrules any negative cards close by it in a spread.

ADVICE: Relax; appreciate your blessings.

REVERSED MEANING: There is no specific negative meaning for the optimistic Sun, other than potential delay to plans.

THE SUN.

XX JUDGEMENT

KEYWORDS: Assessment, second chances, forgiveness, awakening.

With Judgement, we judge ourselves, whereas XI Justice (page 106) judges us. Judgement brings a turning point and an opportunity to revisit the past in order to move on. The angel symbolizes awakening or seeing an old situation in a new light. As memories resurface, you may decide to give a relationship or other past situation a second chance; this may be due to a new spirit of forgiveness, or the broader perspective that time and distance bring. An additional meaning of the card is spiritual connection and receiving messages from guides and loved ones in spirit.

ADVICE: Look back with compassion.

REVERSED MEANING: Judging yourself too harshly or living in the past. Holding on to feelings of regret or shame that could be released.

JUDGEMENT.

XXI THE WORLD

KEYWORDS: Completion, success, reward, joy.

The World marks the successful completion and celebration of a life phase or goal; you have come full circle and are rewarded for achievement in your professional life and relationships. You may also see your horizons expand, with a broader perspective on life or an opportunity to travel to a new destination. The World also suggests togetherness within the self and others; you are at one with the world.

ADVICE: Enjoy your deserved success.

REVERSED MEANING: There is no negative meaning for this joyful card, only that completion and reward may be delayed for a time.

THE WORLD.

The Minor Arcana: Cups

ACE OF CUPS

UPRIGHT MEANING: New love and new passions. Overflowing emotion: joy and blessings. Also, fertility, pregnancy, and the birth of a baby or project.

REVERSED MEANING: Feeling overwhelmed, worries about relationships, fertility issues.

TWO OF CUPS

UPRIGHT MEANING: Love and peace. Happy professional and love partnerships; meeting a soul mate or kindred spirit.

REVERSED MEANING: Trust issues; imbalance or disappointment in a partnership.

THREE OF CUPS

UPRIGHT MEANING: Celebrations, friendship, and flirtation; thriving creatively and emotionally.

REVERSED MEANING: Feeling distanced from support networks; the need to take extra care of yourself.

FOUR OF CUPS

UPRIGHT MEANING: A plateau. Feeling bored or flat; a need to see the good opportunities on offer.

REVERSED MEANING: Stubbornness, cynicism, or deeper boredom; the need for action.

FIVE OF CUPS

UPRIGHT MEANING: Loss and sadness; however, there are still some avenues to explore. Stay positive.

REVERSED MEANING: A period of sadness or instability is ending; look forward to better times ahead.

SIX OF CUPS

UPRIGHT MEANING: A visitor arrives, often a person from the past, bringing happy reminiscences.

REVERSED MEANING: Nostalgia that becomes a refuge rather than a temporary pleasure.

SEVEN OF CUPS

UPRIGHT MEANING: Dreams and possibilities that are not yet manifest; there is much potential, but everything feels up in the air.

REVERSED MEANING: The need to wait for information before making a choice.

EIGHT OF CUPS

UPRIGHT MEANING: It's time to leave an old situation behind; go your own way.

REVERSED MEANING: Feeling abandoned or neglected; poor timing.

NINE OF CUPS

UPRIGHT MEANING: Joy and sharing as wishes come true; love, generosity, and relationship happiness.

REVERSED MEANING: Fixating on a goal that may not be important; alternatively, dealing with others' egos.

TEN OF CUPS

UPRIGHT MEANING: Relationship and family happiness; also, a new home or dream come true.

REVERSED MEANING: Pressure to conform to others' expectations; there's no need.

PAGE OF CUPS

UPRIGHT MEANING: A new friend, love, or idea; creativity, dreaminess, imagination, and fun.

REVERSED MEANING: Relationship issues; misunderstandings and oversensitivity to criticism.

KNIGHT OF CUPS

UPRIGHT MEANING: Romance and opportunity; can indicate new friendships, a proposal, or offer.

REVERSED MEANING: Idealism without foundation; empty promises or commitment issues.

QUEEN OF CUPS

UPRIGHT MEANING: Love and happiness are important to you now; this is a good time for creative projects, and overall, following your intuition and your heart.

REVERSED MEANING: Emotional or financial pressure; demanding or jealous behavior.

KING OF CUPS

UPRIGHT MEANING: Support and love; being open-hearted in the way you communicate. Empathy can resolve differences.

REVERSED MEANING: Vulnerability and defensiveness; dealing with volatile behavior.

The Minor Arcana: Pentacles

ACE OF PENTACLES

UPRIGHT MEANING: A new beginning, such as a new job, business, or home. Brightens any negative minor arcana cards that fall close to it in a spread.

REVERSED MEANING: Financial problems, such as debt or cash flow. Can also show an overly materialistic attitude.

TWO OF PENTACLES

UPRIGHT MEANING: Weighing up options; deciding how to manage money and a choice between locations, jobs, or courses.

REVERSED MEANING: Imbalance in a partnership; commitment or financial issues need careful consideration.

THREE OF PENTACLES

UPRIGHT MEANING: Being appreciated for your work; early success in a venture or project. Also, job interviews, talks, and presentations.

REVERSED MEANING: Unfinished business. Frustration and delay.

FOUR OF PENTACLES

UPRIGHT MEANING: Being financially secure; putting down roots and finding balance; financial challenges are over.

REVERSED MEANING: Becoming too entrenched in routine; clinging to material possessions.

FIVE OF PENTACLES

UPRIGHT MEANING: Loss or isolation, which may be financial or social. However, the card usually reveals fear of losing something, rather than reality.

REVERSED MEANING: Hardship that challenges you; look for support, as you may have more resources than you think.

SIX OF PENTACLES

UPRIGHT MEANING: Money is given to you; it may be a gift, bonus, or other reward. Equally, you may be the giver, generously supporting others.

REVERSED MEANING: Your kindness is not repaid yet, or money due to you is outstanding.

SEVEN OF PENTACLES

UPRIGHT MEANING: The need for continued effort—this situation has great potential, so stay focused on the goal rather than doubting your path.

REVERSED MEANING: Doubt or disillusion; walking away too quickly from a potentially good opportunity.

EIGHT OF PENTACLES

UPRIGHT MEANING: Hard work, perfectionism, and professionalism; solid achievement and reward, plus further development opportunities.

REVERSED MEANING: Feeling overworked and underpaid or underappreciated; it may be time to look for a more rewarding path.

NINE OF PENTACLES

UPRIGHT MEANING: Security and contentment; proud of your achievements, you may give yourself a reward and enjoy some luxury and/or leisure time.

REVERSED MEANING: Materialism, or dealing with overspending; you may feel insecure financially.

TEN OF PENTACLES

UPRIGHT MEANING: Prosperity and family; the happy joining of two families through marriage; generosity, love, and support.

REVERSED MEANING: Miscommunication between generations of a family; issues around money or inheritance.

PAGE OF PENTACLES

UPRIGHT MEANING: An offer, such as new work, education, or a new venture, with opportunities to develop your skills.

REVERSED MEANING: Financial or property issues; meanness; lack of flexibility.

KNIGHT OF PENTACLES

UPRIGHT MEANING: Good financial planning and reward for hard work; also, loyalty and honesty.

REVERSED MEANING: Potential dishonesty, the need to take control of finances, seek trustworthy advice, and check agreements.

QUEEN OF PENTACLES

UPRIGHT MEANING: Generosity and wisdom; solid friendship, comfort, and support; good health and financial security.

REVERSED MEANING: Financial problems—overspending or meanness, or waiting for money owed to be paid.

KING OF PENTACLES

UPRIGHT MEANING: Money and security; trust, generosity, and practical support. Problems are solved.

REVERSED MEANING: Greed and materialism; selfishness and, at worst, fraudulent activity.

The Minor Arcana: Swords

ACE OF SWORDS

UPRIGHT MEANING: A breakthrough or decision that brings success; clear thinking and insight. The card brightens any negative minor arcana cards that appear close to it in a spread.

REVERSED MEANING: A decision goes against you. Feeling dominated or being outwitted.

TWO OF SWORDS

UPRIGHT MEANING: Procrastination or a truce; time to reflect on an upcoming decision. A need to move forward.

REVERSED MEANING: Feeling stuck; not having the information or confidence you need to make a positive choice.

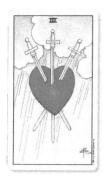

THREE OF SWORDS

UPRIGHT MEANING: Upset and sorrow, which can be due to a third party in a relationship or in your professional life.

REVERSED MEANING: Knowing the truth; releasing emotions to move on.

FOUR OF SWORDS

UPRIGHT MEANING: Time out to recover from stress or illness; taking refuge. In love, a relationship goes on hold.

REVERSED MEANING: An unwelcome interruption to your routine; the need to accept the situation.

FIVE OF SWORDS

UPRIGHT MEANING: An unwinnable battle; feeling defeated. A time to pick yourself up and look forward.

REVERSED MEANING: Feeling humiliated or bullied by a domineering individual.

SIX OF SWORDS

UPRIGHT MEANING: Moving on from problems to peace; a time of unrest is over. You may also travel at this time.

REVERSED MEANING: You can make progress but may need to let go of an attitude or problem first.

SEVEN OF SWORDS

UPRIGHT MEANING: Insecurity; you may need to protect what is yours and be aware of any dishonest behavior.

REVERSED MEANING: Feeling like a victim; there is a danger you may surrender to circumstances rather than hold your position.

EIGHT OF SWORDS

UPRIGHT MEANING: Feeling hemmed in by your thoughts; overthinking and restriction may be the cause, but you can think your way out.

REVERSED MEANING: Strong emotions such as fear or guilt may make you feel frustrated or oppressed; this too will pass.

NINE OF SWORDS

UPRIGHT MEANING: Anxiety and stress disturb your peace; try to let go of any underlying fear and trust that the situation will improve.

REVERSED MEANING: Feeling alone; ask for support, as you do not have to suffer in silence.

TEN OF SWORDS

UPRIGHT MEANING: A swift and sudden ending. This may be unexpected, but you can now move on.

REVERSED MEANING: A need to cling to the past; try to accept things as they are now.

PAGE OF SWORDS

UPRIGHT MEANING: Agreements and contracts; the need to pay close attention to detail and have your wits about you.

REVERSED MEANING: Sniping and underhandedness; tactlessness.

KNIGHT OF SWORDS

UPRIGHT MEANING: Unpredictability, opposition, and conflict; the need for calm resolution.

REVERSED MEANING: Mind games and drama; a battle that is best abandoned.

QUEEN OF SWORDS

UPRIGHT MEANING: Independence, intelligence, and strength; often, a single woman with great strength of character.

REVERSED MEANING: Obsessiveness and unfair treatment; ruthless attitudes.

KING OF SWORDS

UPRIGHT MEANING: Ambition and decisions, which may be legal or official; being judged; taking strong, swift action.

REVERSED MEANING: Being overruled or dominated by a headstrong opponent.

The Minor Arcana: Wands

ACE OF WANDS

UPRIGHT MEANING: Good news and beginnings; inspiration, movement, and travel. Fertile ideas and children.

REVERSED MEANING: Miscommunication and delay; potential fertility issues.

TWO OF WANDS

UPRIGHT MEANING: A new partnership; plans take shape. Travel or new creative ideas beckon.

REVERSED MEANING: Delays to plans and potential doubt concerning love or professional partnerships.

THREE OF WANDS

UPRIGHT MEANING: Travel, success, and potentially new love. Creativity and self-expression.

REVERSED MEANING: The need for patience; delays may frustrate you, but success is coming.

FOUR OF WANDS

UPRIGHT MEANING: Feeling happy and free. The card can show the return to childhood haunts, a new relationship, and the honeymoon phase.

REVERSED MEANING: Delays may affect your plans; these may be frustrating, but they are temporary.

FIVE OF WANDS

UPRIGHT MEANING: Competitions and tests; the need to stand your ground and make sure you are heard.

REVERSED MEANING: A need for discretion; you may be surrounded by people who are untrustworthy or being casual with the truth.

SIX OF WANDS

UPRIGHT MEANING: Success and validation, particularly in tests, examinations, and personal projects.

REVERSED MEANING: Victory is coming; your reward may be delayed, but keep up the effort.

SEVEN OF WANDS

UPRIGHT MEANING: Standing your ground. Stay true to your values and purpose, and you will succeed.

REVERSED MEANING: Feeling locked in an ongoing dispute, or having to continually defend yourself.

EIGHT OF WANDS

UPRIGHT MEANING: Events speed up, with news, communication, and travel; stuck situations take a leap forward. Also, good news concerning relationships.

REVERSED MEANING: Frustration due to delays and misunderstanding or lack of communication.

NINE OF WANDS

UPRIGHT MEANING: Strength, but also overvigilance; being wary of opposition. You may need to let go a little to free up ideas and energy.

REVERSED MEANING: Becoming defensive because you have had to be strong for a long time.

TEN OF WANDS

UPRIGHT MEANING: Losing perspective; you may be overloaded with responsibility just now. It's time to prioritize rather than agree to every demand.

REVERSED MEANING: Pressure; feeling habitually overwhelmed. As with the upright card meaning, it is time to step back.

PAGE OF WANDS

UPRIGHT MEANING: Good news, particularly concerning projects and new ideas; assess each offer before you commit. Also, can predict a happy reunion.

REVERSED MEANING: Confusion and miscommunication; being distracted, or not being heard.

KNIGHT OF WANDS

UPRIGHT MEANING: Making progress; stuck issues get resolved and a romance may begin. Can also reveal moving home.

REVERSED MEANING: Plans may be put on hold, leading to frustration; also, someone may be unclear as to their goals or even insincere.

QUEEN OF WANDS

UPRIGHT MEANING: Dynamic self-expression; a great time to get projects under way and communicate ideas.

REVERSED MEANING: Creative block, or other temporary delays to plans and projects.

KING OF WANDS

UPRIGHT MEANING: Confidence and leadership; being open to new people, ideas, and experiences. Being the initiator.

REVERSED MEANING: Overconfidence; a lack of listening and sharing. Feeling silenced or unable to express yourself.

CHAPTER

6

Numerology

Numerology is the art of number interpretation. Numbers are believed to have unique energetic signatures, which have meaning—and these meanings reveal much about your future potential and character.

In modern numerology, we primarily use the numbers 1 through 9, each of which has a unique vibration. Numbers 11 and 22, known as master numbers, are also included, as it's believed they have an intense vibration: 11 and 22 may mean you have a deep calling and the potential to make a significant contribution, although certain sacrifices may be needed along the way.

So, in total, there are 11 number profiles given, but you have more than one number. Numerology gives you a way to calculate a whole series of numbers that reflect your inner and outer selves, and to help you to divine your future prospects.

How to Calculate Your Numbers

All you need is your date of birth and your name, from which you can calculate your Life Path number, Destiny number, Soul number, and Personality numbers; it's a matter of adding together the numbers in your birth date, reducing them to a single digit (or in some cases, including 11 and 22), and looking up the numbers equivalent to the letters in your name. We use the whole name to calculate the Destiny number, only the consonants for the Personality numbers, and just the vowels for the Soul number—so your name alone holds a set of key numbers that unlock a meaning just for you.

Your Life Path Number: Life Direction

Your Life Path number is the sum of all the numbers in your date of birth, reduced to 1–9, 11, or 22. It reveals your life direction, showing how you might progress.

For example:

Date of birth: October 29, 1976

$1 + 0 + 2 + 9 + 1 + 9 + 7 + 6 = 35$

$3 + 5 = 8$

So the Life Path number for this person is 8.

Also, take note of any repeating numbers in the date of birth. In this example, we have:

1 0 2 9 1 9 7 6

There are two number 9s, so 9 would be a secondary Life Path number, with 8 being the dominant number. In this case, you would look up both 8 and 9 in the number interpretations.

Your Destiny Number: Life Lessons

Your Destiny number is the sum of numbers equivalent to your full name on your birth certificate, reduced to 1–9, 11, or 22. This number tells you about the lessons you learn throughout life. See the chart below to work out how all the letters in your name translate into numbers.

1	2	3	4	5	6	7	8	9
A	B	C	D	E	F	G	H	I
J	K	L	M	N	O	P	Q	R
S	T	U	V	W	X	Y	Z	

Example:

Full name: PAUL DAVID MASON

PAUL = 7 + 1 + 3 + 3 = 14; 1 + 4 = 5

DAVID = 4 + 1 + 4 + 9 + 4 = 22; 2 + 2 = 4

MASON = 4 + 1 + 1 + 6 + 5 = 17; 1 + 7 = 8

5 + 4 + 8 = 17

1 + 7 = 8

Therefore, Paul's Destiny number is 8.

Your Soul Number: Your Deeper Self

Your Soul number is the sum of numbers equivalent to the vowels in your full name on your birth certificate, reduced to 1–9, 11, or 22. The Soul number signifies your deeper self and your intuitive desires.

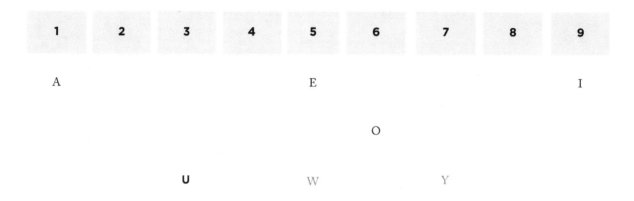

1	2	3	4	5	6	7	8	9
A				E				I
					O			
		U		W		Y		

Example:

Full name: LAUREN TATE

LAUREN = 1 + 3 + 5 = 9 (counting only the vowels A, U, and E)

TATE = 1 + 5 = 6

9 + 6 = 15

1 + 5 = 6

So, Lauren's Soul number is 6.

Note that W and Y also count as vowels, but only in certain instances.

• Y is a vowel when it is sounded as an I, for example in Bryn; and when it comes after a vowel and informs that vowel's sound, such as in Hayford (the Y makes the long a sound).

• W is a vowel when it comes after a vowel and informs that vowel's sound, as in Jewell or Howard.

Your Personality Numbers: Facets of Your Personality

Personality numbers are calculated by adding up numbers equivalent to the consonants in your full name, acquired name(s), and nickname(s). These numbers reflect the different faces you show to the world—at work and in personal relationships, for example. Add together the consonants' numbers for each name and write them down.

1	2	3	4	5	6	7	8	9
	B	C	D		F	G	H	
J	K	L	M	N		P	Q	R
S	T		V	W	X	Y	Z	

Example:

Work name: Samantha

1 + 4 +5 + 2 + 8 = 20 (counting only the consonants S, M, N, T and H)

2 + 0 = 2

Friends and family name: Sam

1 + 4 = 5

Name used for freelance photography business: Samantha Fry

1 + 4 + 5 + 2 + 8 + 6 + 9 = 35

3 + 5 = 8

Note that the Y in Fry does not count as a vowel, so we only include the F and R in the surname.

At work, Samantha is a 2; with friends and family, a 5; and in her freelance photography work, an 8. One interpretation would be that in her day job, Samantha's success depends upon cooperation and strong working partnerships (2), while her freelance business is a platform for great future achievement (8). As a 5 with friends and family, she shows the freedom-loving side of her personality, enjoying trips away, connecting easily with others, and being willing to take risks.

The Numbers

The Number 0

Zero expresses both nothing and all the other numbers; zero symbolizes infinite possibility. It cannot come up as one of your personal numbers, but it is worth noting if it appears in your date of birth. For example, if you were born on 10/10/2000, you would have five zeros, more than any number. This may indicate you have an all-or-nothing attitude and strong views. Also, given that nothing, or zero, is the goal of Zen, you may have a spiritual or philosophical nature.

Number 1: The Monad—Innovation

One represents light and the primal aspect of God or Source, symbolized by a dot within a circle, a concept attributed to the Pythagoreans. One is the number of unity, deity, and divine intelligence. One denotes oneness with the divine, singularity, action, beginnings, and opportunities. Ones are believed to be highly individual character types.

Symbol: A dot in the center of a circle

Best days of the month for 1 as Life Path: 1st, 10th, 19th, 28th

Character influences: Ones are tenacious, focused, and single-minded. You can achieve great things because you are motivated to make things happen your way. You do not rely on others to fulfill all your needs, and you are willing to step out alone, which means taking certain risks. You may be a visionary entrepreneur, a leader, or simply someone who wishes to live in a way that suits you, regardless of pressure to conform. Because you have such a strong sense of self, others lean on you. Although you do not invite attention or seek power, you support others and will take on huge responsibility if the situation requires it. One also symbolizes divinity and Oneness with the universe. You nurture your own relationship with spirit.

Shadow character: Intolerance and stubbornness; disinterest in others' opinions or advice; arrogance.

Advice: Have courage. Go your own way.

Number 2: The Duad—Empathy and Cooperation

Two is the number of equality and unity in diversity. Diversity encompasses the idea of two opposites, equality, justice, and fairness—seeing both sides of a situation. Twos often seek balance and harmony and have great empathy for others.

Symbol: The line (two points joined together)

Best days of the month for 2 as Life Path: 2nd, 11th, 20th

Character influences: Twos are inherently kind, with a high level of sensitivity to others. Twos thrive on social interaction and succeed professionally because they see both sides of a situation and make fair and honest assessments. In their personal lives, they may take on a challenging or unsuitable partner or friend because they prefer to see the best in people, even when this means they give more than they receive. They may avoid conflict and expend much time and energy healing others' hurts. Making friends and new contacts comes easily to a Two, because they prioritize relationships and will always support and defend those they love.

Shadow character: Overgiving; giving too much weight to others' opinions; fearing judgment.

Advice: Trust your intuition rather than feeling obliged to others.

Number 3: The Triad—Energy and Expression

Three was regarded as the perfect number by ancient philosophers. A symbol of fulfillment, the triangle was the subject of Pythagoras's famous theorem; he also taught that three expressed the nature of the universe as Matter, Idea, and God. Three is the number of energy, enthusiasm, optimism, and fulfillment. Threes are often dynamic, expressive character types.

Symbol: The triangle

Best days of the month for 3 as Life Path: 3rd, 12th, 21st, 30th

Character influences: Threes prize creativity and freedom, and you organize your life accordingly—so you can pursue what truly fascinates you. This makes for a roller-coaster existence, riding high one minute and feeling lost the next, but the optimistic Three recovers quickly, begins again, and is often successful. You need stimulation and distraction, so regular nine-to-five office work may not suit; you may prefer to travel for work or run your own projects or business. Threes are also great communicators and may excel at persuasion or direct selling, provided you believe in what you are offering.

Shadow character: Impulsiveness, overconfidence, impatience; lack of staying power.

Advice: Admit mistakes and see balance as a goal rather than a compromise.

Number 4: The Tetrad—Willpower and Order

Four denotes stability, structure, order, and willpower; it also signifies the four elements of Fire, Earth, Air, and Water. Fours are loyal and practical character types who focus on creating lasting emotional and financial security.

Symbol: The square

Best days of the month for 4 as Life Path: 4th, 13th, 22nd, 31st

Character influences: Order is important to a Four type, so you prefer to follow rather than flout the rules and work in environments in which conventional structures are essential to achievement. At work and at home, you do not turn away from tough work and the jobs others will not do, because you understand the value of these tasks in the greater scheme of supporting the whole. You may find fulfillment in spiritual service and enjoy being part of a large organization or network. Whatever your age, professional status, or time limitations, you do whatever needs to be done efficiently. Working as part of a team adds to your feeling of security. In relationships and friendships, Fours are outstandingly loyal and honest.

Shadow character: Lack of initiative; fussiness, martyrdom; difficulty adapting to new people or surroundings.

Advice: It's fine not to follow every rule; do things your way, too.

Number 5: The Pentad—Expansion and Freedom

Five is the number of vitality, discovery, and the five senses. Five character types tend to be sensual, with great energy and curiosity.

Symbol: Pentagon, five-pointed star, or pyramid

Best days of the month for 5 as Life Path: 5th, 14th, 23rd

Character influences: Fives are the ultimate multitaskers, who try many things; you may not succeed in every challenge you take on, but what counts is the adventure. You thrive on tests of courage and can be led by your heart. Fives may have many passionate affairs and often have lots of good friends, as you easily connect with others and are genuinely interested in their lives. In your professional life, you make a great strategist; perceptive and fast-acting, you know how best to respond to a problem or opportunity. Fives also have the ability to make the most of any situation and often appreciate the simpler things in life.

Shadow character: Casual thoughtlessness, lack of consideration; irresponsibility.

Advice: Bring your focus to one or two goals and consistently pursue them.

Number 6: The Hexad—Love and Protection

Six is the number of happiness, love, and idealism. It also denotes harmony, due to its geometric shape—the hexagon is perfectly balanced. Sixes are loving and seek a peaceful life. They aim to act for the higher good and are often sensitive and imaginative.

Symbol: The hexagon, the Seal of Solomon (two intersecting triangles)

Best days of the month for 6 as Life Path: 6th, 15th, 24th

Character influences: The charitable Six enjoys giving to others and is motivated by love and the need for peaceful, caring relationships. If you have money, you are excited by what it can do to support those you love, how it might contribute to your community, and how it may help those who are less fortunate; wealth otherwise means little. This does not mean you are unambitious, however. You may be strongly motivated by creative projects, for example, but the goal is never financial. In relationships, you are loyal and caring, and you take your responsibility to others seriously.

Shadow character: Being too idealistic; neglecting good financial opportunities.

Advice: Avoid those who mistake your kindness for weakness.

Number 7: The Heptad—Mystery and Wisdom

Seven is the number of knowledge, self-discipline, mystery, and fate. Sevens often have great wisdom and the resilience to stand by their ideas.

Symbol: The heptagon

Best days of the month for 7 as Life Path: 7th, 16th, 25th

Character influences: Sevens are associated with philosophy, wisdom, and imagination. Small concerns may not be of interest to you; your remit is the mysteries of this world and what is beyond. Intellectually ambitious, you may be ahead of your time. As a result, you become strong, enduring the pain of being rejected or misunderstood, but you know you can contribute to society through the knowledge you have acquired, and have the determination to stand by your beliefs. You may be naturally reserved and recharge best in your own company.

Shadow character: Being overcritical; neglecting friendships; impracticality.

Advice: Focus on putting your knowledge into practice; manifest your ideas.

Number 8: The Ogdoad—Power and Success

Eight is the number of power in the material world. Eights are excellent organizers who achieve their goals.

Symbol: The cube (which has eight corners)

Best days of the month for 8 as Life Path: 8th, 17th, 26th

Character influences: Eights are practical, powerful, and determined to succeed; they often have a flair for business and are fast to react to an opportunity. Their focus is stability, but Eight character types can also embrace change because they respond brilliantly to it, reorganizing and adapting to create the security they value. They are kind and loving but tend not to fall in and out of love, because this invites disruption; they prefer to nurture a deep, constant bond with a long-term partner. In friendships, they are giving and supportive but know where to draw the line if they feel they are being manipulated.

Shadow character: Being domineering; tactlessness; overly materialistic.

Advice: Listen to others' opinions; deepen your understanding.

Number 9: The Ennead—Spirituality and Courage

Nine is the number of intensity, courage, spirituality, genius, and boundaries. It is the last single-digit number before 10, said to hold the preceding numbers within itself. Nines are often inspired, highly intelligent people.

Symbol: The nonagon (nine-sided shape)

Best days of the month for 9 as Life Path: 9th, 18th, 27th

Character influences: The Nine personality is similar to that of number Seven—both types are cerebral, but the Nine has the advantage of genius. As a Nine, you may be the ideal mentor, consultant, counselor, or adviser, and you have the potential to make an outstanding contribution to your field of work. Success comes due to your inspiring ideas and sharp intellect, so you may rise quickly in your chosen profession. The Nine has the gift of discernment and knows how and where to direct his or her energy and attention. You are a supportive, sympathetic, and loyal friend, just like the Six.

Shadow character: Lack of focus; inconsistency; inability to complete anything.

Advice: With sustained effort, anything is possible.

Master Numbers

Numbers 11 and 22 are believed to have intense vibrations. These types are often associated with having an evolved awareness.

Number 11: Intuition

Eleven can be considered a doubly empowered One. As Ones are associated with leadership, ingenuity, and communication, at the level of Eleven, the influence of the One expands into global communities and can also signify great faith. Elevens are believed to be visionary and charismatic individuals.

Character influences: Eleven people often possess a special gift in a chosen subject area and a unique power of communication. You have the ability and drive to articulate your ideas, and you can passionately convince and motivate others. You have strong beliefs and values, and you'll often put a cause above your own needs, making personal sacrifices in order to help others. Some Elevens are clairvoyants and healers and/or creative and artistic. You may feel a deep call to be of service to the world.

Shadow character: Overidentifying with a cause; lack of perspective; obsessiveness.

Advice: Temper your idealism so your goals remain realistic.

Number 22: Global Vision

Twenty-Two is known as the number of the master builder. It adds up to Four, the number of stability and structure, so whatever the Twenty-Two makes is designed to last. It may also be impressive, even a legacy for future generations. Twenty-Twos are therefore associated with power and the realization of a vision.

Character influences: Twenty-Two people materialize ideas; whatever you envision, you make. It is important that you see results, so you may direct your energies into a physical product, building, or other environment that represents your values and beliefs. Equally, you may put together a group or evolve a larger organization or business that delivers a service or lasting benefit to others. Twenty-Twos are therefore highly sensitive to others' needs, with great empathy and compassion.

Shadow character: Stubbornness; lack of attention to important detail; intense anger.

Advice: Stay within reasonable boundaries; you don't need to push so hard.

CHAPTER

7

Scrying with a Crystal Ball

Scrying can be immensely rewarding if we accept whatever we sense and receive. This is a challenge; after all, we believe we're supposed to physically "see" in reflective surfaces. But if we see a surface as a gateway to our inner eye, we discover a powerful technique for self-connection and divinatory knowing. Scrying can also heighten your visual and sensual awareness, benefiting other divination practices.

Choose a Ball

You can work with any size ball. Crystals with inclusions and clouds are perfect, as the light we use to read with illuminates these features, creating a fantastical stage for our intuition. The crystals below are those associated with crystal-gazing, but you can choose any crystal ball or flat crystal with which you sense a connection.

Crystals and Their Divinatory Qualities

CRYSTAL	HELPS ACTIVATE
Amethyst	Spiritual connection; psychic ability
Aquamarine	Spiritual connection; perspective
Citrine	Intuition; manifesting
Clear quartz	Clarity; spiritual connection; manifesting
Fairy quartz	Faery connection; practical guidance
Labradorite	Intuition; psychic ability
Lemurian quartz	Angelic connection; oneness; accessing ancient wisdom
Obsidian	Spiritual growth; past lives
Rose quartz	Love and relationships; compassion
Rutilated quartz	Channeling; manifesting
Selenite	Angelic connection; stability
Smoky quartz	Groundedness; patience

Crystals and the Days of the Week

Monday	Selenite
Tuesday	Clear quartz
Wednesday	Citrine
Thursday	Amethyst, aquamarine
Friday	Rose quartz
Saturday	Obsidian, labradorite
Sunday	Rutilated quartz

Timing Your Relationships

Meditating on an object—a crystal ball, or a flat, smooth crystal—triggers a change in consciousness; we shift from our everyday reality into the imaginal, intuitive realm. We might sense or directly see colors or shapes. You may find an image develops on the surface of the crystal, or you see with your inner vision, receiving an image in your mind.

When to Scry

There are several timing traditions, but overall, be guided by that pull of anticipation: whenever you sense a question building and feel that it is time to ask. If you feel connected with the moon, you can also choose a time when the moon is increasing (waxing), as this represents a situation or energy growing. One tradition suggests you begin a scrying session just before twilight, which is associated with occult manifestations. You can also choose the day of the week that is associated with the particular crystal you are working with (see page 138).

Timing and Recording Your Sessions

Begin by timing yourself for one minute, then three, then five. When you begin, scrying can feel intense, so set a timer to limit your sessions. As you become more comfortable, build up to five minutes, or longer if it feels right. It is also helpful to do your mystic gazing in the same place and at the same time each day, as this helps build connection with your crystals or ritual.

After a session, journal what you experienced, or draw what you saw or sensed, and review it as events unfold.

Preparation: Making a Connection

You will need a crystal ball, some dark cloth or a dark surface, a candle, and a notebook or paper. Choose a candle that is shorter than your crystal ball so the light or flame you use will shine through most of the crystal (you'll set your light behind your crystal ball). Keep the notebook or paper and pen to hand, because you might prefer to jot down impressions during your gazing session for reflection later.

1. Cleanse your crystal ball by bathing it in moonlight for several consecutive nights or using one of the methods listed on page 10. Do not cleanse it by placing it in direct sunlight, as this poses a fire hazard.

2. You'll need to work in a quiet room with subdued lighting (bright sunlight or bright indoor lighting creates reflections on the crystal's surface). Lower or turn off the lights.

   Sit comfortably and set your intention; holding your crystal, take a breath and ask it to work with you for your higher good. Ask, also, for any necessary protection during the reading; you can visualize yourself in a bubble of white light. This traditional protection method guards against any negative influences and is particularly important when scrying with old mirrors.

continued

3. Keep holding your crystal ball, sensing a growing connection between you and your crystal. Close your eyes and see what you sense, feel, and see. It's important to do this, particularly if you are a beginner; looking directly into a crystal without preparation can in some cases block the intuitive pathway because the expectation that we should immediately "see" an image sets up resistance to openness.

4. Now open your eyes and, still holding your crystal, gaze into its surface; visualize the crystal taking you on a journey. Sense the vibration of the crystal in your hands and allow any sensations to arise without asking a question. Tune in to your senses: You might get flashes of color, sensations in your body, such as a light tingling; or you may simply feel peaceful. Take at least five minutes just to be with your crystal in this way, opening up a channel of communication between you.

How to Begin Scrying

5. Place your crystal ball on its stand, light a candle or switch on your tealight or flashlight app, and place the light source behind the crystal ball. Move the light around, still behind the ball, until the position feels right. You may begin to see images forming and changing as you move the light. Areas that appeared cloudy without illumination now begin to have depth. Slowly turn the ball around on its stand; again, you will see the crystal landscape change. Let the ball rest in the position that you sense is right, to begin; you can continue to move the crystal and light source throughout the reading.

6. When you are ready, consider your question. You may prefer to ask the crystal for insights into a situation or for general guidance. Speak your question aloud or silently up to three times, then gaze into your crystal. You can do this:

   • With your eyes open

   • With your eyes half-shut, so the crystal becomes soft-focus

   • With your eyes closed; you may find that you naturally close your eyes and see mental images

Stay relaxed and don't consciously try to see. Blink whenever you need to, rather than fix a stare. Find a focal point within the crystal: This might be an inclusion, a spot where light refracts, a tiny fracture within the crystal, or a cloudy area. Keep your breathing slow and steady. If any extraneous thoughts distract you, just observe them and let them go, returning to your focal point. The more relaxed you feel, the easier it is for you to recognize images and sense messages from your crystal when they arise.

What Do You See?
The Meanings of Symbols and Colors

Symbols are traditionally said to appear on the right of the crystal ball, but they can appear anywhere (and you may receive them in your mind rather than through an image on the ball). Here are some conventional interpretations:

- **Rising clouds:** Yes in answer to a question
- **Descending clouds:** No
- **Waning moon (a C-shape):** Decrease and possible loss
- **Waxing moon (a mirror-image C):** Growth and prosperity
- **Heart:** Love
- **Ship or plane:** Travel

For other symbols, use the list of tea leaf symbols (see pages 52–59). Above all, interpret any symbols you see in your own way. You may also find you hear messages rather than literally see colors and symbols; if you do, write them down.

Take note of any colors you see. The traditional meaning of colors in scrying are as follows, but you may have your own.

- **Red:** Danger
- **Orange:** Anger
- **Yellow:** Challenges
- **White:** Positive energy, protection
- **Blue:** Success
- **Green:** Happiness, health
- **Black and gray:** Negative energy

Light shades of any color apart from gray—pink, lemon, or lilac, for example—are considered positive. Overall, though, interpret the colors in terms of how you respond to them, rather than adhere to standard color interpretations.

You may hear words during scrying. Some practitioners do not see images but get names or messages; others experience bilocation, the feeling of being in two places at once.

Ending the Session

When you have finished scrying, thank the crystal for its messages, take a breath, and bring yourself back to the present moment. Wrap your crystal in dark cloth and place it in a safe place, away from light, to protect its energy. Extinguish or turn off the candle.

About the Author

Liz Dean

Liz Dean is a tarot teacher and professional tarot reader in private practice and at Psychic Sisters within Selfridges, London. A former commissioning editor in illustrated book publishing, Liz is the author of seventeen books and card decks, including HBO's *Game of Thrones Tarot*, *The Ultimate Guide to Tarot*, *The Ultimate Guide to Tarot Spreads*, *The Art of Tarot*, *Fairy Tale Fortune Cards*, *The Victorian Steampunk Tarot*, and *Switchwords: How to Use One Word to Get What You Want*. She is a former coeditor of *Kindred Spirit*, the United Kingdom's leading spiritual magazine. Her work has been featured in the national UK press, including *Spirit & Destiny* and the *Daily Express*.

WWW.LIZDEAN.INFO

WWW.SWITCHWORDSPOWER.COM

Index

agate, 15
   blue lace, 15
   fire, 15
   moss, 16
air hand, 64
Algiz, 31, 39
amazonite, 16
amber, 16
amethyst, 17
Ansuz, 31, 33
Apollo, mount of, 69
aquamarine, 17
aventurine, green, 18

Berkana, 31, 40
bloodstone, 18

carnelian, orange/red, 18
casting stones, 11
celestite, blue/white, 19
Celtic Cross, 99
Chariot, 104
children lines, 90
chirognomy, 63–74
chiromancy, 75–91
citrine, 19
colors, scrying and, 141
cross, palmistry and, 91
crystal ball
   about, 137
   choosing, 138
   ending session, 141
   how to begin, 140
   meanings and interpretation of,
     141
   preparation for, 139–140
crystals
   about, 9
   cleansing, 10
   meanings of, 15–27
   techiques for, 11–14
Cups, 94, 112–114

Dagaz, 31, 43
Death, 107
decision reading, 45
Destiny Number, 127
Devil, 108
Duad, 131

earth hand, 64
Ehwaz, 31, 41
Eihwaz, 31, 38
Elder Futhark, 30–43
emerald, 19
Emperor, 103
Empress, 102
Ennead, 134

Fate, goddesses of, 44
fate line, 75, 83–84
Fehu, 31, 32
fingers
   fingertip markings, 66
   gaps and, 74
   interpreting, 73–74
   leaning, 74
   length of, 65, 72
   see also hands; palmistry
fire hand, 64
Fool, 101
Frey's Aett, 30–35

garnet, red, 20
Gebo, 31, 35
girdle of Venus, 89
global vision, 135
great triangle, 91
grid of destiny, 47
grille, palmistry and, 91

Hagalaz, 31, 36
Hagalaz's Aett, 30–31, 36–39
hands
   mounts of, 68–71
   position, texture, and color of, 64
   shapes of, 64
   zones of palm, 66–67
   see also fingers; palmistry
Hanged Man, 107
head line, 75, 79–80
health line, 86
heart line, 75, 81–82
Heptad, 133
Hermit, 105
Hexad, 133
Hierophant, 103
High Priestess, 102

Inguz, 31, 42
intention, setting, 11
intuition
   line of, 87
   numerology and, 135
Isa, 31, 37

jade, green, 20
jasper
   red, 20
   yellow, 21
Jera, 31, 37
jet, 21
Judgement, 111
Jupiter, mount of, 70
Justice, 106

Kaunaz, 31, 34
Kings, 94, 114, 117, 120, 123
Knights, 94, 114, 117, 120, 123

labradorite, 21
Laguz, 31, 42
lapis lazuli, 22
life line, 75, 77–78
Life Path Number, 126
Lovers, 104

Magician, 101
major arcana, 94, 101–111
major lines
   about, 75
   fate line, 75, 83–84
   head line, 75, 79–80
   heart line, 75, 81–82
   life line, 75, 77–78
   timing and, 76
malachite, 22
Mannaz, 31, 41
marriage lines, 87
Mars
   line of, 88
   mount of (inner), 70
   mount of (outer), 70
   plain of, 71
master numbers, 135
Mercury, mount of, 69
merged mounts, 71
minor arcana, 94, 112–123

minor lines, 76, 85–90
Monad, 130
Moon (card), 110
moon, mount of, 71
moonstone, 22
mystic cross, 91

Nauthiz, 31, 36
nine-rune cast, 46
Norns, 44
numerology
    about, 125
    calculating numbers, 126–129
    master numbers, 135
    meanings and interpretation of,
        130–134

obsidian
    Apache tear, 23
    black, 23
Ogdoad, 134
onyx, 23
opal, blue, 24
Othila, 31, 43

Pages, 94, 114, 117, 120, 123
palm
    major lines on, 75–84
    minor lines on, 76, 85–90
    other markings on, 91
    prints of, 75
    zones of, 66–67
palmistry
    about, 61
    chirognomy, 63–74
    chiromancy, 75–91
    finger lengths, 65
    hand position, texture, and color,
        63
    hand shapes, 64
    learning to read hand and palm, 62
    left- and right-hand meanings, 62
past, present, future readings, 14, 98
Pentacles, 94, 115–117
Pentad, 132
peridot, green, 24
Personality Number, 129
Pertho, 31, 38
plain of Mars, 71

quartz
    clear, 24
    rose, 25
    rutilated, 25
    smoky, 25
Queens, 94, 114, 117, 120, 123

Raido, 31
rascettes, 89
relationships, timing, 88, 139
rhodonite, 26
runes
    about, 29
    decision reading, 45
    Elder Futhark, 30–43
    grid of destiny, 47
    meanings and interpretation of,
        31–43
    nine-rune cast, 46
    reading, 44–47
    three Norns, 44
    types of, 30

Saturn, mount of, 70
scrying
    about, 137
    choosing a ball, 138
    ending session, 141
    how to begin, 140
    meanings and interpretation of,
        141
    preparation for, 139–140
    timing of, 139
selenite, white, 26
Skuld, 44
sodalite, 26
Soul Number, 128
Sowelo, 31, 39
square, palmistry and, 91
Star (card), 109
stars, palmistry and, 91
Strength, 105
Sun, 110
sun line, 85
sunstone, 27
Swords, 94, 118–120

tarot cards
    about, 93
    choosing cards, 96

cleansing, 100
Cups, 94, 112–114
deck structure and, 94
how to begin, 94
Kings, 94, 114, 117, 120, 123
Knights, 94, 114, 117, 120, 123
major arcana, 94
meanings and interpretation of,
    100–123
minor arcana, 94
Pages, 94, 114, 117, 120, 123
Pentacles, 94, 115–117
Queens, 94, 114, 117, 120, 123
reversed cards, 96
shuffling question into, 95
Swords, 94, 118–120
techiques for, 97–100
Wands, 94, 121–123
tea
    about, 49
    interpreting cup, 51
    reading leaves, 50
    symbols for, 52–59
Temperance, 108
Tetrad, 132
Thurisaz, 31, 33
tiger's eye, brown-gold, 27
Tiwaz, 31, 40
tourmaline, black, 27
Tower, 109
Triad, 131
triangles, palmistry and, 91
turquoise, 27
Tyr's Aett, 30–31, 40–43

Urd (Wyrd), 44
Uruz, 31, 32

Venus
    girdle of, 89
    mount of, 71
Verdandi, 44

Wands, 94, 121–123
water hand, 64
week ahead reading, 100
Wheel of Fortune, 106
World, 111
Wunjo, 31, 35

yes-no readings, 12